BLACK LIVES
GREAT MINDS OF SCIENCE

WRITTEN BY
TONYA BOLDEN

ILLUSTRATED BY **DAVID WILKERSON**

Abrams Fanfare • New York

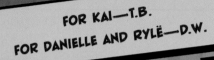

FOR KAI—T.B.
FOR DANIELLE AND RYLË—D.W.

Library of Congress Control Number 2023952530
ISBN 978-1-4197-5269-8
eISBN 978-1-64700-215-2

Text © 2024 Tonya Bolden
Illustrations © 2024 David Wilkerson
Book design and lettering by Charice Silverman

Printed and bound in China
10 9 8 7 6 5 4 3 2 1

ABRAMS The Art of Books
195 Broadway, New York, NY 10007
abramsbooks.com

CONTENTS

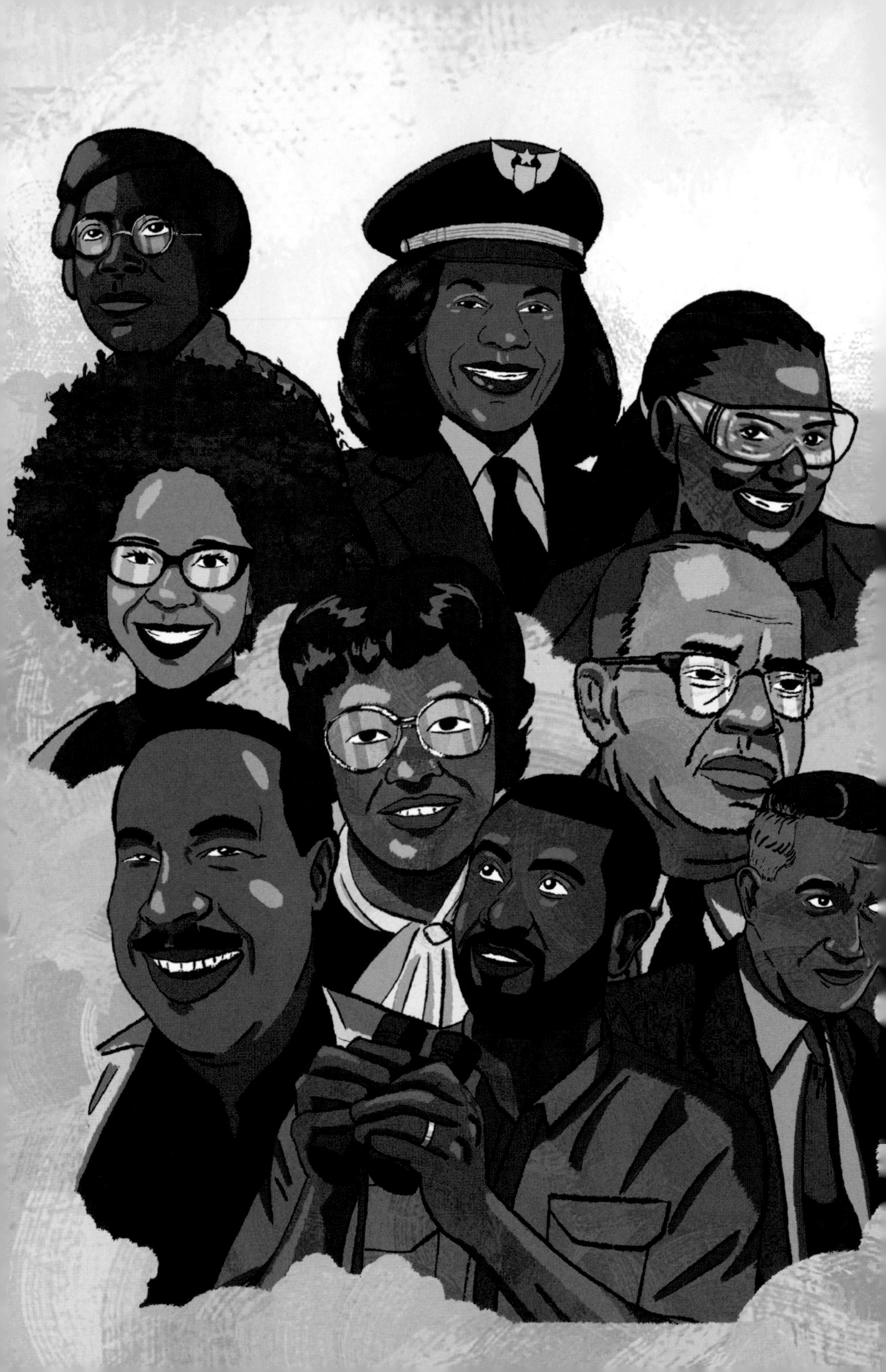

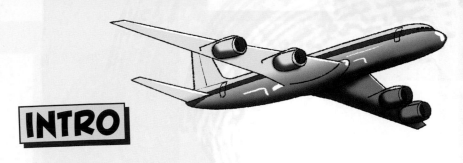

INTRO

Hey there!

Welcome to the first installment in a graphic nonfiction series that dives into the lives of awesome achievers in a range of fields.

People from different eras.

People from different places.

People who followed their passions and met with deep-down satisfaction.

The series aims, yes, to introduce (or reintroduce) you to some fascinating folks, but it also seeks to kindle your curiosity about various professions—make you want to learn more. And, who knows, you just might find the profession that is the perfect fit for you.

Enjoy!

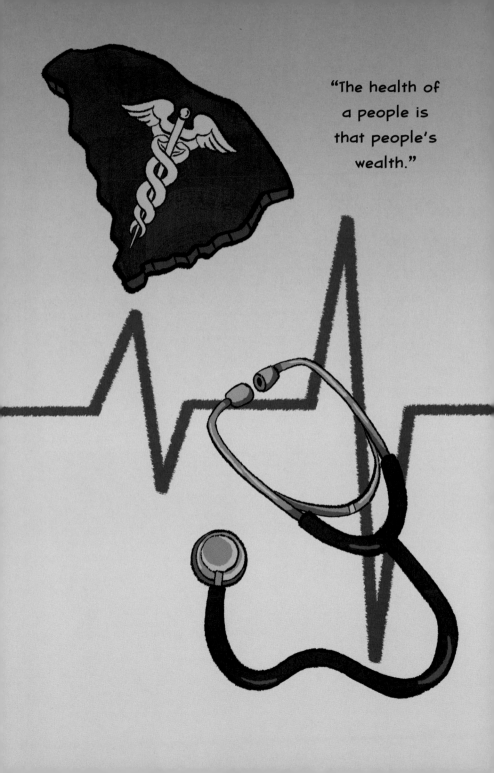

"The health of a people is that people's wealth."

MATILDA EVANS

PHYSICIAN

DEDICATED. DEVOTED. DETERMINED.

That was Matilda Arabella Evans, a native of Aiken, South Carolina, greatly influenced (and nurtured) by an uncle who was an herbalist and a grandmother who was a nurse and midwife.

Had it not been for them young Matilda's play might never had included, as one source tells us, "steeping leaves to make medicines, rolling bits of clay into pills, and practicing on chickens she caught running about the ground."

THE NUMBERS

When Dr. Evans graduated from medical school there were about 130,000 doctors in the nation. Roughly 7,000 were women.

An all-grown-up Matilda wanted to do more than play at medicine, and she eventually summoned up the pluck to enroll in the Woman's Medical College of Pennsylvania (WMCP) in Philadelphia, founded in 1850, and one of the first medical schools in the world for women.

Matilda entered WMCP in 1893 when the overwhelming majority of doctors were white men.

WMCP, 1893

In 1897, after she made the grade in anatomy (the study of the structure of the body), embryology (the study of unborn babies), histology (the study of the body's tissues), obstetrics (the branch of medicine focused on pregnant women and childbirth), pathology (the study of injuries and diseases), and other science courses, Matilda was one of WMCP's 26 graduates.

After graduation, Matilda A. Evans, MD, headed down to Columbia, South Carolina, about 50 miles from her hometown and where she became the second Black woman licensed to practice medicine in the Palmetto State.

This was at a time when most Black people there had little to no access to health care. The hospital in Columbia, for example, wouldn't take Black patients. (By the way, the first Black woman licensed to practice medicine in South Carolina was Lucy Hughes Brown, who graduated from WMCP in 1894.)

7

In Columbia, Dr. Evans hung out her shingle in a house on Lady Street, charging 50 cents to $1.50 for office visits. Like most doctors back then, she made house calls—traveling by bike, on horseback, and sometimes in a horse-drawn buggy or wagon. (It wasn't until around 1912 that she bought a car—a spiffy white Buick.)

While Dr. Evans was on her mission to improve the health of her people, she became the physician of choice for a number of wealthy white women in Columbia and the surrounding area. At a time of intense racism and sexism, Dr. Evans also gained the respect of male physicians, Black and white.

Being a physician wasn't enough for her. In 1901 she opened Taylor Lane, a combined hospital and nursing school. And she managed to get white doctors to work at her hospital.

"I HAVE DONE WELL AND HAVE A VERY LARGE PRACTICE AMONG ALL CLASSES OF PEOPLE."

Dr. Evans was definitely eager to see more Black women become doctors. In 1907 she wrote to a WMCP official, Alfred Jones, rooting for a woman who had attended her nursing school to get a scholarship. She also updated Jones on her own progress.

A 1910 article in Columbia's white-owned newspaper, *The State*, hailed Dr. Evans as "South Carolina's brainiest" Black person and reported that Black people "without a penny in their pockets come for treatment to the Taylor Lane from a radius of 130 miles around Columbia."

No one was ever turned away because they couldn't pay and whatever a patient could offer instead of cash she apparently happily accepted. That same article in *The State* reported that three Black women had recently offered "a half dozen eggs, a basket of peas, and a small bag of home raised peanuts" in exchange for treatment.

How was Dr. Evans able to keep Taylor Lane afloat?

Handsome fees from her wealthy patients.

Donations large and small from people near and far who applauded her work.

Plus, she had her side hustles. One was selling vegetables grown on a three-acre farm behind her hospital, where tragedy struck in the spring of 1911: Taylor Lane was consumed by flames.

Dr. Evans was not defeated. In 1914 she had another hospital and nursing school, St. Luke's, up and running and kept it open until sometime in 1918, when she joined the Volunteer Medical Service Corps. (This was during World War I and an influenza pandemic.)

After that, Dr. Evans carried on with her private practice. And in the 1920s, on her 20-acre farm, she opened Lindenwood Park, where kids (along with grown-ups) could swim, dance, and enjoy other healthy forms of recreation.

Matilda also rallied folks to help her open a free clinic for children.
   Some people donated a dollar. Others donated five dollars. Still others donated a lot more. Reverend J. P. Reeders and his congregation donated the basement of their church, Zion Baptist. That's where the institution soon called the Evans Clinic opened in July 1930.

On opening day, Dr. Evans, her assistants, and a handful of teachers who had volunteered to pitch in were expecting maybe 200 young clients. Instead more than 700 children showed up!—many on crutches and scores showing signs of malnourishment.

On day two, "even more children," said *The State*, "swarmed about the church" and on day three "the crowd was so great that traffic on the street was brought to a standstill."

"THE HEALTH CONDITIONS AMONG OUR PEOPLE IN THE CITY IS ALARMING. I WAS DISTRESSED TO FIND SO MANY CHILDREN UNDER WEIGHT, UNDER NOURISHED, AND ACTUALLY SUFFERING FOR THE LACK OF SOME SIMPLE TREATMENT THAT WOULD GIVE BETTER HEALTH."

The Evans Clinic soon moved to a building on the corner of Harden and Lady Streets. In March 1931 the Black-owned *Palmetto Leader* reported that the clinic even had a kindergarten and described Dr. Evans as a woman possessed of "an all consuming passion for alleviating suffering and ills, especially among the poor and neglected."

Several months later, *The State* had this to say of the Evans Clinic: "The rooms and furnishings are spotlessly clean; the window panes shine; the floors are dustless and there is about the whole establishment and those who are connected with it a spirit of enthusiasm and earnestness which augurs well for its future."

That future included even larger premises on Taylor Street, right across the street from Dr. Evans's home.

And it was there in 1935 that Dr. Matilda Arabella Evans passed away, after nearly 40 years of steadfast service to her community. During that time the good doctor had adopted several children (some were bloodkin and some had been abandoned at one of her hospitals). Dr. Evans had also been a foster parent to more than twenty children.

MAY 13, 1872 born Matilda Evans in Aiken, South Carolina.

CA. 1885 began her first formal education in Aiken at a school founded by Pennsylvania-born Martha Schofield, a white Quaker and former abolitionist.

1887–1891 attended the preparatory department of Oberlin College in Oberlin, Ohio, with funds Schofield raised and by working odd jobs.

1892–1893 taught at a school founded by a Black woman (Lucy Laney), Haines Institute, in Augusta, Georgia, then worked at Schofield's school in Aiken.

1897 graduated from Woman's Medical College of Pennsylvania.

1916 founded the Negro Health Association of South Carolina and went on to edit its *Negro Health Journal of South Carolina*, a short-lived weekly newspaper that educated folks on how to take better care of themselves.

1922 served as president of the all-Black Palmetto Medical

DR. EVANS REMEMBERED

★ In 1993 Columbia's Richland Memorial Hospital (later the Prisma Health Richland Hospital) gave out its first Dr. Matilda A. Evans Award, given annually to an outstanding Black healthcare professional.

★ In 2019 a historical marker was placed at 2027 Taylor Street where Dr. Evans lived from 1928 until her death in 1935.

★ In 2020 Columbia's Williams Drive was renamed Matilda Evans Street.

★ In 2022 South Carolina's General Assembly and Senate passed resolutions recognizing and praising Dr. Evans for her years of service to South Carolinians.

Association, when no other Black woman headed a state medical society. She later served as a regional vice president of the National Medical Association, the first organization representing Black healthcare professionals.

NOVEMBER 17, 1935 died in her home.

"First comes the dream when you are an engineer, then a vision of your dream appears. The excitement mounts, it's almost breath-taking and you can hardly wait to put it down on paper. When you do, those are the plans. All the time you can't sleep, you can't eat. All you want to do is get the plans in concrete and steel."

ARCHIE ALEXANDER

CIVIL ENGINEER

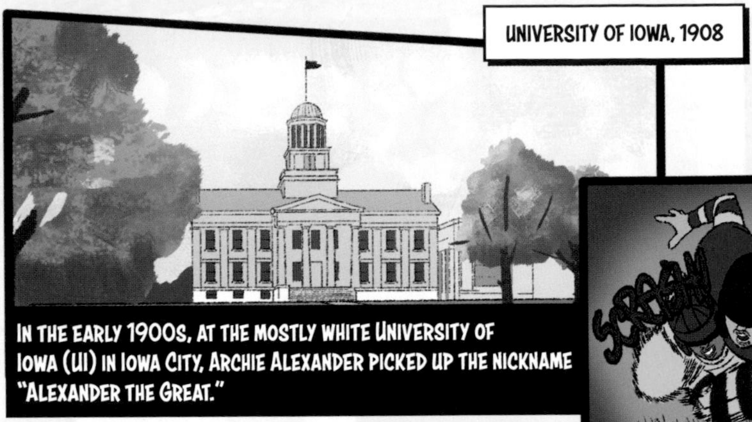
UNIVERSITY OF IOWA, 1908
IN THE EARLY 1900S, AT THE MOSTLY WHITE UNIVERSITY OF IOWA (UI) IN IOWA CITY, ARCHIE ALEXANDER PICKED UP THE NICKNAME "ALEXANDER THE GREAT."

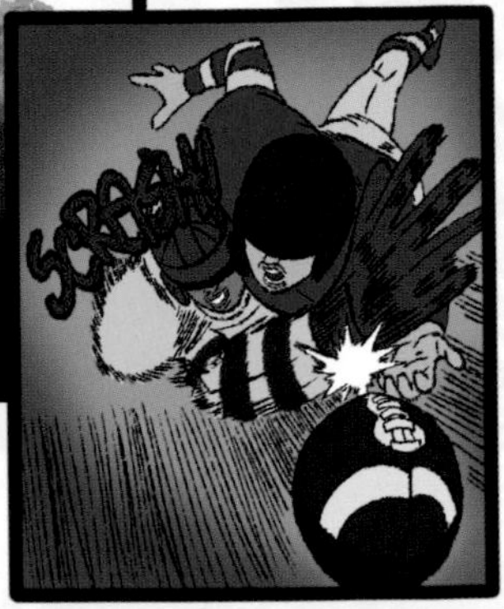

That was for his talent as tackle on the varsity football team.

But greatness on the gridiron wasn't his highest ambition. This six-foot-two, 180-pound young man yearned, above all, to design and build things!

"NEVER MIND THAT THE DEAN OF UI'S ENGINEERING SCHOOL TOLD ME THAT MY PURSUIT WAS 'A WASTE OF TIME.' NEVER MIND THAT A PROFESSOR TOLD ME THAT ENGINEERING WAS A 'TOUGH FIELD' AND LIKELY 'TWICE AS TOUGH' FOR A BLACK PERSON."

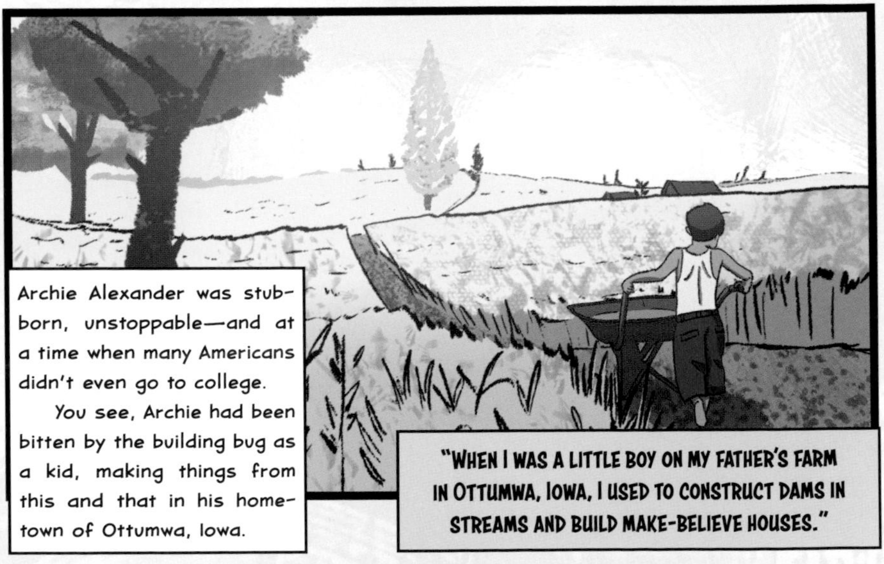
Archie Alexander was stubborn, unstoppable—and at a time when many Americans didn't even go to college.
You see, Archie had been bitten by the building bug as a kid, making things from this and that in his hometown of Ottumwa, Iowa.
"WHEN I WAS A LITTLE BOY ON MY FATHER'S FARM IN OTTUMWA, IOWA, I USED TO CONSTRUCT DAMS IN STREAMS AND BUILD MAKE-BELIEVE HOUSES."

Chances are young Archie kept building things after this family moved about 100 miles north of Ottumwa to Saylor Township, then to nearby Des Moines. There, after graduating from Oak Park High, he went to Highland Park College—but for only a year. By the time his sophomore year rolled around, the school had decided to ban Black students.

After this insult Archie Alexander made tracks for UI, where he certainly had his work cut out for him. Required courses for civil engineering included mathematics, physics, surveying, geology, mechanics, hydraulics, electrical engineering, structural design, and drawing. His senior thesis, or research project, was a design for a reinforced concrete viaduct to replace the wooden bridge over Iowa City's College Street railroad tracks.

I DID IT!

On June 12, 1912, Alexander the Great, who had worked a variety of part-time jobs to pay for college, became the first Black person to graduate from UI's engineering school.

After that triumph, though Alexander searched high and low, he had no luck landing a job as a civil engineer, so he took one as a drafter in Des Moines, at the Marsh Engineering Company, where he had worked some summers.

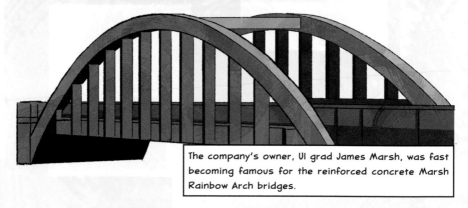

The company's owner, UI grad James Marsh, was fast becoming famous for the reinforced concrete Marsh Rainbow Arch bridges.

Alexander started out at Marsh's earning $10 a week. Two years later, he was at $70 a week and supervising bridge construction in Iowa and Minnesota.

The ever-ambitious Archie Alexander then launched his own firm in Des Moines, A. A. Alexander Inc., with his heart set on designing and building bridges! bridges! bridges!

No luck.

Repairing a chimney.

Small paving jobs.

That was the only kind of work he was able to hustle up, but he did what he always did: stayed determined.

Things eventually picked up to the point that Alexander took on a junior partner, George Higbee, a white engineer he'd worked with at James Marsh's firm.

At a time when interracial firms of any kind were rare and frowned upon by many people, Alexander & Higbee met with success. Some of the contracts this new firm snagged early on included ones for building bridges in the Iowa townships of Bangor, Liscomb, and Marietta.

The firm did well enough for Alexander to take a break and travel to Europe. In his passport application he said he planned to study and travel in England, France, and Italy. Many sources say that he studied bridge design at the University of London.

A few years later, in the spring of 1925, Alexander's business partner died after a horrible accident on a construction site in Iowa City.

George Higbee was felled by a beam. His injuries included a skull fracture and a crushed chest and right arm.

Archie Alexander carried on as sole proprietor. Winning the contract to build a new College Street bridge in Iowa City, the subject of his thesis, had to have been a super thrill.

UI: POWER PLANT, 1927

During these days, his biggest project wasn't a bridge. In the late 1920s, UI hired him to construct several facets of its heating system, including a new power plant.

When it came to his construction crews, Archie Alexander didn't care about race, only about skills.

And he was a real stickler about safety. When a reporter asked Al McLaughlin, a white foreman, why Alexander's firm had few accidents and delays on construction sites, McLaughlin explained that it was because "all the machinery, from shovels to cranes and concrete mixers, is brought new every eighteen months."

He added that his boss "just isn't the sort of a man to be bothered by breakdowns and he won't have anything but new machinery."

Other workers had nothing but high praise for Archie Alexander, who, said that same reporter, went about jobsites with "a pack of blue prints in his hands and a gleam in his eyes."

Hailed as one of the "leading contract engineers in Iowa and the Midwest," Archie Alexander soon teamed up with Maurice Repass, a white friend. Repass had also graduated from UI's engineering school in 1912 (and had also played football).

In years to come Alexander & Repass did great!, great!, great! The firm's primary focus? You guessed it—bridges!

One was the Union Pacific Railroad deck-plate girder bridge over the North Platte River in Nebraska. Another, the steel stringer East 14th Street Viaduct in Des Moines. Alexander's firm also built bridges in Illinois, Oklahoma, Michigan, Missouri, and Minnesota.

Projects outside the Midwest included Washington, D.C.'s granite-and-limestone Tidal Basin bridge and seawall, with its spectacular springtime view of the cherry blossom trees that ring the reservoir. The work, which cost more than $1 million (about $23 million in today's dollars), was completed in 1943 (and the bridge was later named the Kutz Memorial Bridge).

Four years later, during UI's celebration of its 100th anniversary, Archie was one of the 100 alums honored for their "high attainment in their chosen fields of endeavor." By then the school had about 30,000 graduates.

"THAT WAS THE PROUDEST MOMENT IN MY LIFE."

TIMELINE

MAY 14, 1888 born Archibald Alphonso Alexander in Ottumwa, Iowa.

1912 earned his bachelor's in civil engineering from the University of Iowa.

1914 launched his first company, A. A. Alexander, Inc.

1917 took on George Higbee as a junior partner.

1926 received the Harmon Foundation Award for outstanding achievement in business and engineering.

1929 took on Maurice Repass as a junior partner.

CA. 1940 with wife, Audra, took a trip to Egypt, where he beheld some of the most famous engineering marvels in the world: the Pyramids!

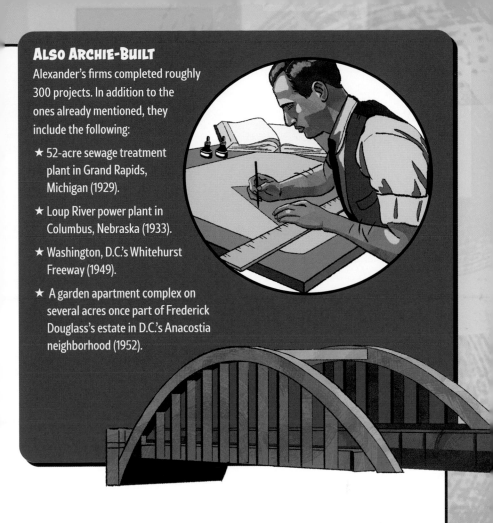

Also Archie-Built

Alexander's firms completed roughly 300 projects. In addition to the ones already mentioned, they include the following:

★ 52-acre sewage treatment plant in Grand Rapids, Michigan (1929).

★ Loup River power plant in Columbus, Nebraska (1933).

★ Washington, D.C.'s Whitehurst Freeway (1949).

★ A garden apartment complex on several acres once part of Frederick Douglass's estate in D.C.'s Anacostia neighborhood (1952).

1944 won in a court case the right to purchase a fabulous six-bedroom Tudor revival home at 2200 Chautauqua Parkway in one of Des Moines's upscale all-white neighborhoods that had banned Black people from living there.

JANUARY 4, 1958 died in Des Moines, Iowa.

"There are three ways for you to become successful. First, don't be afraid to get your hands dirty. Don't be afraid to work. Try lots of jobs. Work for nothing if you have to, but get the experience. You never know when what you have learned will come in handy.

Second, you have to read. Find out what others know. You don't have to buy books. Use libraries! . . .

And third, you have to believe in yourself."

FRED JONES
INVENTOR

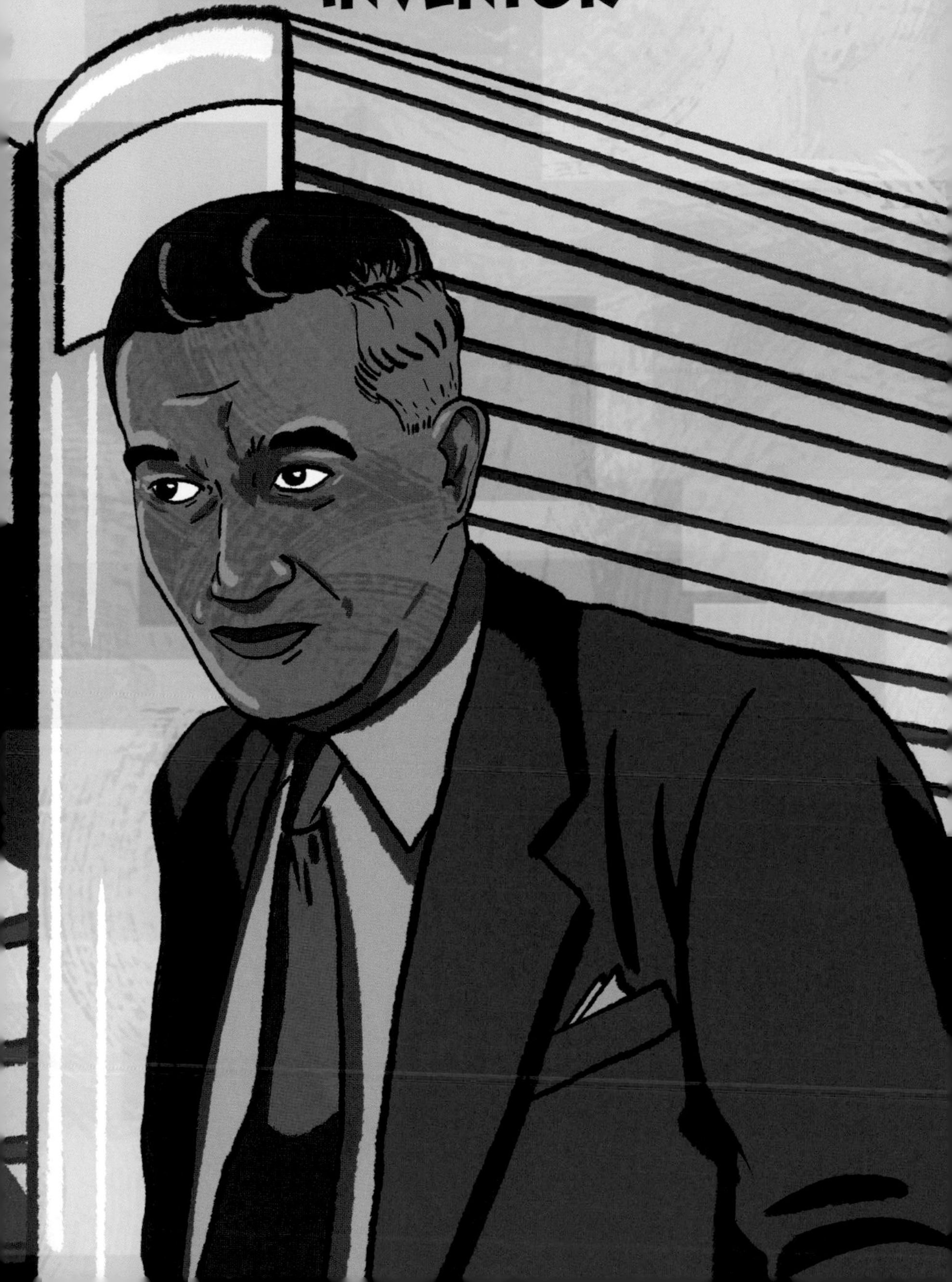

"BORN HANDY" IS THE TITLE OF A 1949 *SATURDAY EVENING POST* MAGAZINE PIECE ON JONES, WHO AT AGE FIVE, LEGEND HAS IT, TOOK APART A POCKET WATCH TO SEE WHAT MADE IT TICK TOCK AND THEN PUT IT BACK TOGETHER.

That watch belonged to Fred's father, John, a white Irishman who repaired railroad tracks and who was raising the boy solo. (Fred never knew his mother.)

One day John Jones took his little tinkerer and his meager belongings from their home in Covington, Kentucky, across the Ohio River to Cincinnati, Ohio. There, he put his son in the care of a Catholic priest, Father Ryan, who had agreed to let Fred live in the rectory and see to it that the lad went to school while his father searched for work.

Fred, age seven, never laid eyes on his daddy again.

When the orphaned boy wasn't in school, wasn't earning his keep—scrubbing floors, mowing grass, shoveling snow, chopping firewood, cooking—he was often hanging out with Oscar, a chauffeur for a family that had *two* automobiles—a sedan and a touring car—at a time when the majority of Americans still got about by horse and buggy.

IF YOU WANT TO EAT, YOU WORK!

Oscar let Fred help him keep those cars clean and shiny. Plus, when one needed repair he let the boy ride along to R. C. Crothers's Garage. The sight of the place—the tools, the equipment, the cars—blew Fred's mind.

At age 12 he ran away from Father Ryan and eventually talked R. C. Crothers into giving him a job.

"AND I REMEMBER IT WAS A FRIDAY AND HE SMILED AND SAID HE GUESSED HE COULD TRY ME OUT ON MONDAY. BUT DO YOU THINK I'D WAIT THREE DAYS TO GET MY HANDS ON THOSE CARS? . . . I WAS DOWN THERE AT SIX A.M. SATURDAY, WAITING FOR HIM TO COME AND OPEN UP THE PLACE."

Fred went from helper to expert mechanic to foreman of that garage by age 15. And he was soon designing and building "speed wagons" for his boss to drive in local races.

Following a falling-out with Crothers,
Fred Jones moved from place to place.

Washed dishes here.

Chopped wood there.

In St. Louis he tended the boiler of a paddle wheel steamboat.

In Chicago he was a mechanic at the Cadillac garage.

In Effingham, Illinois, the owner of Pacific House, a hotel, hired him to fix his old furnace—something Jones had never done before. But he figured it out!

"I HALF EXPECTED THAT OLD BOILER TO BLOW UP THE HOTEL! BUT LUCK WAS WITH ME. IT KEPT HEATING UP, AND THE FLUE PIPES DIDN'T LEAK, AND THE STEAM STARTED WARMING THE HOTEL. THAT JOB GAVE ME A LOT OF CONFIDENCE."

Fred Jones went on to be real handy on a 30,000-acre farm near Hallock, Minnesota. He kept the tractors and other farm equipment running right. He did the same for his boss's four cars, one of them a classy Packard Roadster. And Jones didn't stop at being a mechanic. He became a skilled electrician, too. Always poring over technical books and magazines, he became an all-around Mr. Fix-It for his neighbors.

After he landed a job at a garage in Hallock, he built a race car for himself—*Number 15*—one that beat out an airplane on the 500-foot track at the fairgrounds. He later built a new and improved *Number 15*, which he raced in various states.

What's more, in the mid-1920s, when "talkies" were replacing silent films, Jones devised for the town's Grand Theatre a sound system that was cheaper than those already on the market.

Word of Jones's handiwork reached Joe Numero of Minneapolis, Minnesota, who owned a company that made sound equipment for movie theaters. Soon, Jones had a full-time job at Numero's firm, making improvements on sound equipment. Jones also invented a machine for dispensing movie tickets and any change customers might be due.

Then one day, after a friend of Numero's got some terrible news, Jones invented something way cooler.

That friend of Numero's was Harry Werner, who owned a trucking company. The terrible news was that one of his trucks with a cargo of 35,000 pounds of raw chicken had broken down on its way from the Twin Cities to Chicago. The ice keeping the cargo cool melted and all that chicken—rotten!

Werner got the news during a golf game with Numero in late spring 1938. Also there was Al Fineberg, head of an air-conditioning company.

Joe Numero turned to Jones to tackle the problem. Knowing a thing or two about making things vibration proof from his days building race cars, Jones got to work.

His first refrigerator unit, mounted beneath the trailer, worked! But, boy, was it heavy—some 2200 pounds—plus it got splattered with dirt and other road debris.

"A BIG CLUNK."

Still, before the year was out, Numero had a new company, Thermo Control. He was in the business of making refrigeration units for long-haul trucking with Fred Jones as his chief engineer.

Jones stayed at the drawing board until he came up a much lighter unit, one mounted up top—and Thermo Control really took off.

Thanks to Fred Jones's invention, folks in, say, New York could get fresh fruits and vegetables from California, some 3,000 miles away. Companies that made frozen foods—from vegetables to ice cream—had reason to ramp up production. And with a wider variety of food available year-round, more small grocery stores became supermarkets.

"More than 5,000 trucks and trailers, operating on highways from Alaska to Argentina and even in Greece and Arabia, are now equipped with Thermo Control refrigerators," reported the author of that 1949 *Saturday Evening Post* piece "Born Handy."

By then Fred Jones was vice president of Thermo Control, and he had invented other refrigeration units, including ones used by the U.S. armed forces during World War II (units for cooling field hospitals for example). The ever-innovating Jones went on to design technology to keep food and other perishables cool while traveling by plane, ship, and train freight car.

KING OF COOL

In 1961, the year that Fred Jones died, Numero sold his company to Westinghouse Electric Company for roughly $35 million. By then the company had been renamed Thermo King.

Fred Jones, later dubbed "The King of Cool," never got rich from his inventions. He never applied for a patent on most of his early ones, which meant that other people could use them without paying him a dime. As for patents on his dozens of refrigeration-related inventions, they belonged to Joe Numero.

TIMELINE

MAY 17, 1893 born Frederick McKinley Jones in Cincinnati, Ohio.

1918–1919 served in the segregated U.S. Army during World War I. Stationed in France, he was plenty handy, from rewiring camps to repairing motorcycles and trucks.

1944 became the first Black person elected to the American Society of Refrigeration Engineers.

KING OF COOL

While in Hallock, Jones didn't only invent things for the Grand Theatre. He also invented . . .

★ A snowmobile made out of airplane and automobile parts to speed doctors to and from house calls on wintry days.

★ One of the first portable X-ray machines for the town's hospital.

1953 a Black community center in Minneapolis, named after Phillis Wheatley, presented him with its merit award "for outstanding achievements which serve as an inspiration to youth."

FEBRUARY 21, 1961 died in Minneapolis.

1977 inducted into the Minnesota Inventors Hall of Fame.

1991 first Black person awarded the National Medal of Technology and Innovation, the highest U.S. honor for technical innovation. This award was bestowed by President George H. W. Bush.

2007 dedication of Thermo King's Frederick McKinley Jones Research and Development Center in Minneapolis. By then Thermo King was owned by Ingersoll Rand, which had bought the company from Westinghouse in 1997 for $2.56 billion.

"It's strange; I almost can't believe it. I didn't think so many people would ever be interested in my story or that GPS would go so far and develop into what it is today."

GLADYS B. WEST

MATHEMATICIAN

IMAGINE A DEVICE THAT COULD ALLOW CONSERVATIONISTS TO TRACK WILDLIFE; HELP METEOROLOGISTS WITH WEATHER FORECASTS; ENABLE PEOPLE IN MOTION, FROM HIKERS AND BIKERS TO DRIVERS, TO GET FROM POINT A TO POINT B WITHOUT A PAPER MAP.

No need to imagine. It's here—and has been for a while. And these are just some of things people can do thanks to GPS (Global Positioning System), the U.S. government-owned technology that provides people all over the world with PNT services (positioning, navigation, and timing) thanks to a network of satellites orbiting Earth.

Gladys B. West played a critical role in the development of this technology.

Not bad for someone whose early education in the 1930s was at a one-room school in rural Virginia—a school with a roof that often leaked, creaky floorboards, worn-out benches, and hand-me-down books from white schools (books that sometimes had missing pages).

44

Gladys's school, Butterwood, was about a three-mile walk from her family's farm in Sutherland, Virginia, where she chopped wood, fed chickens, and did fieldwork along with house chores.

As much as she loved and respected her parents, Gladys knew that the farming life was not for her! **WHAT WAS?**

Her path to a career in math began at Dinwiddie Training School, a high school about 17 miles from her home. (At least there was a school bus.)

At Dinwiddie, Gladys fell in love with geometry, the branch of mathematics that's about the measurement and relationships of angles, points, lines, surfaces, and solids. She became fascinated with geometry because of Mr. Lee, a very dynamic teacher. He made the subject fun!

GEOMETRY comes from the Greek words gē ("earth") and metron ("measure").

HE EVEN RELATED IT TO FARMING, SUCH AS MEASURING THE INCLINES OF THE LAND, AND HOW THE KNOWLEDGE OF ANGLES AND DEGREES COULD POSSIBLY MAKE A FARMER'S JOB EASIER.

Geometry teacher Mr. Lee and other teachers cheered Gladys on—told her that she was "college material." Her spirit really soared when a guidance counselor said that if she finished first or second in her class, she could win a scholarship to attend one of the historically Black colleges in Virginia.

"I WAS TOLD BY MY TEACHERS THAT AN EDUCATION IN MATH OR SCIENCE WOULD LEAD TO MORE OPPORTUNITIES IF I CHOSE IT, SO I DID."

Gladys took on that challenge, graduated first in her class, and was off to Virginia State College (now University) in Petersburg, ready to major in mathematics—ready to tackle tough courses in algebra, geometry, trigonometry, and calculus, for example.

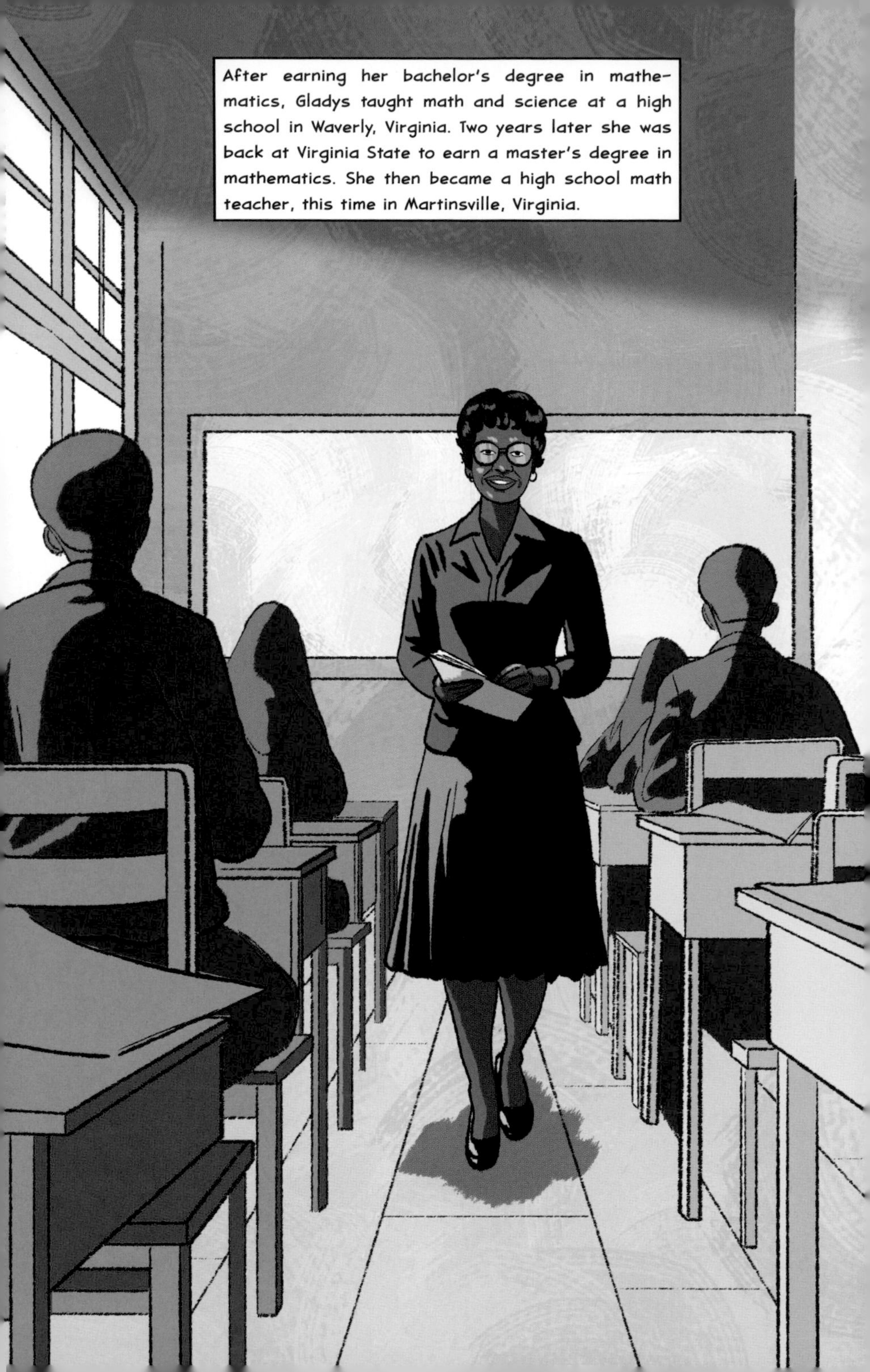
After earning her bachelor's degree in mathematics, Gladys taught math and science at a high school in Waverly, Virginia. Two years later she was back at Virginia State to earn a master's degree in mathematics. She then became a high school math teacher, this time in Martinsville, Virginia.

By then Gladys had applied to several government agencies for a job as a mathematician. Shortly after she started teaching in Martinsville, she heard back from what is today the Naval Surface Warfare Center Dahlgren Division, in Dahlgren, Virginia.

When Gladys went to work at Dahlgren in 1956, she was one of only four Black people (all mathematicians) among its dozens of employees in the sciences. For someone who had spent her life in nurturing Black communities, being at Dahlgren was like being on another planet.

Another big adjustment: switching from a mechanical calculator to an electronic computer.

After a crash course in computer programming, this brainy Virginian worked on range tables, calculating the angles of elevation various weapons had to be set to in order to hit certain targets. She made those calculations on the IBM Naval Ordnance Research Calculator (NORC), the first supercomputer, a machine capable of carrying out 15,000 calculations a second.

Today we have computers that can carry out *trillions* of calculations a second.

"THIS MACHINE, THE SIZE OF AN ENTIRE ROOM, WAS INTIMIDATING TO SAY THE LEAST . . ."

Gladys B. West was later a member of a five-person team that programmed NORC for Project 29V. After 100 hours of computing that involved 5 billion calculations, the team proved that for every two orbits that Pluto makes around the Sun, Neptune makes three.

CONNECTIONS
Ira West was one of the Black mathematicians working at Dahlgren when Gladys arrived. They married in 1957.

West went on to work on a project that involved some 50 mathematicians and engineers, a project that would radically alter life on Earth. She did that work on an even faster computer: the IBM 7030, nicknamed STRETCH.

With STRETCH the team worked on calculations related to artificial satellites orbiting Earth in order to come up with a mathematical model of the shape of Earth, which isn't a perfect sphere. West programmed complex algorithms that used math to create a model of Earth. Without that model, GPS wouldn't be accurate.

When launched in 1978, GPS was strictly for use by the Department of Defense: to enable the military to pinpoint its assets all over the world, from soldiers on the ground to aircraft carriers on the seas. GPS became completely open for civilian use in 1993.

Five years later, after working at Dahlgren for 42 years, Gladys West retired. By then she had earned yet another degree: a master's in public administration.

What's more, she had started work on a PhD in the same field, but then, a few months after she retired, she suffered a stroke.

After recovery, West forged on. In 2000, at age 70, she had that PhD.

It wasn't until years later that the world learned of Gladys B. West's contribution to the development of GPS. Once the story of this "hidden figure" broke, the accolades and awards poured in!

TIMELINE

OCTOBER 27, 1930 born Gladys Mae Brown in Sutherland, Virginia.

1952 earned her bachelor's in mathematics from Virginia State.

1955 earned her master's in mathematics from Virginia State.

1956 started her career at Dahlgren.

1964 received an Award of Merit for Group Achievement along with the other members of the Project 29V team.

1973 earned her master's in public administration from the University of Oklahoma.

1998 retired from Dahlgren.

ALSO DEFINITELY HIDDEN NO MORE!

Margot Lee Shetterly shined the spotlight on four amazing mathematicians in her 2016 book *Hidden Figures: The American Dream and the Untold Story of the Black Women Who Helped Win the Space Race* (the basis for the movie *Hidden Figures*).

One of the women still alive at the time was West Virginia–born **Katherine G. Johnson** (born in 1918). Highlights from her incredible 33-year career at NASA's Langley Research Center in Hampton, Virginia, include calculations vital to *Apollo 11*'s mission to and from the Moon, where, on July 20, 1969, astronauts Neil Armstrong and Edwin "Buzz" Aldrin made history as the first people to walk on the lunar surface.

Hurrahs for Katherine G. Johnson include . . .

★ Presidential Medal of Freedom (2015).

★ A $23 million, 37,000-square-foot NASA research center at Langley named the Katherine G. Johnson Computational Research Facility (opened in 2017).

★ Congressional Gold Medal (2019).

★ An uncrewed resupply spacecraft named the SS *Katherine Johnson*. It first journeyed to the International Space Station on February 20, 2021, 362 days after Johnson passed away at age 101.

2000 earned her PhD in public administration and public affairs from Virginia Tech.

2018 inducted into the Air Force Space and Missile Pioneers Hall of Fame.

2021 received the Prince Philip Medal from the UK's Royal Academy of Engineering and the Pioneer in Tech Award from the National Center for Women & Information Technology.

2023 honored at the Inaugural Black Tie Gala of the National Center of Women's Innovations.

"I wanted to fly airplanes
because I wanted to travel
and see the world."

PATRICE CLARKE WASHINGTON

AVIATOR

IT WAS CAREER DAY AT PATRICE FRANCISE CLARKE'S HIGH SCHOOL IN NASSAU, THE BAHAMAS.

While other girls in her twelfth-grade class spoke of wanting to become nurses or teachers or secretaries—all fine occupations—Patrice announced that she wanted to be an airplane pilot.

The classroom ballooned with laughter.

"EVEN MY FRIENDS LAUGHED."

This was in the late 1970s, when lots of young people (like lots of grown-ups) thought that being an airplane pilot was a career only for men. But Patrice didn't feel bound by stereotypical gender roles. She was raised by a divorced mom and didn't grow up with any brothers, only two younger sisters.

WHATEVER HAD TO BE DONE, MY MOM, I AND MY SISTERS HAD TO DO IT.

With mom working six days a week, the daughters learned to do whatever needed to be done to keep their home in tip-top shape—from cleaning and house painting to yard work and taking out the trash.

But life wasn't all work for the family. Treats included plane trips to nearby Miami for shopping and for vacations. Patrice had her first adventure with these short flights by the time she was four.

Years later, in the article "Soaring to New Heights," *Ebony* magazine had this to say about that first flight: "She remembers being so mesmerized by her window to the world that she only tore herself away from it just long enough to get the plastic pilot wings the flight attendant bestowed upon her and the other kids on the trip."

"MY FAMILY FLEW A LOT BETWEEN NASSAU AND MIAMI SO, GROWING UP, I WAS ALWAYS ON AN AIRPLANE."

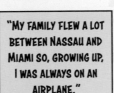

Plane ride after plane ride to and from Miami—*Behold!* a dream was born!

EMBRY-RIDDLE

After high school, Patrice was off to Daytona Beach, Florida, to attend the world-renowned Embry-Riddle Aeronautical University. There, her early days were quite an adjustment. Everything was new, different.

And her first day on campus was far from sunny. It was a cold, bleak January day. Gray sky. Bare trees.

MY GOD, WHAT HAVE I GOTTEN MYSELF INTO?

Patrice knew not a soul at the school, one that didn't have a whole lot of Black students—nor a lot of female ones. What's more, so many students were better prepared for college in America than she was.

But she wanted to see the world and to embrace all that was new and different. **WHAT TO DO?**

AERONAUTICS comes from the Greek words aero ("air") and nautikē ("navigation").

PRESS ON!

Pressing on at Embry-Riddle meant making the grade in a slew of courses, including Aviation History, Flight Rules and Regulation, Instrument Flight, Meteorology, Physics, and Chemistry.

Flight training?
There was Primary and Solo Flight, Cross-country, Twin-engine, Instrument, Emergency Abnormal Maneuvers Training and more in preparation for the Private, Commercial, Instrument and Twin-engine Certifications.

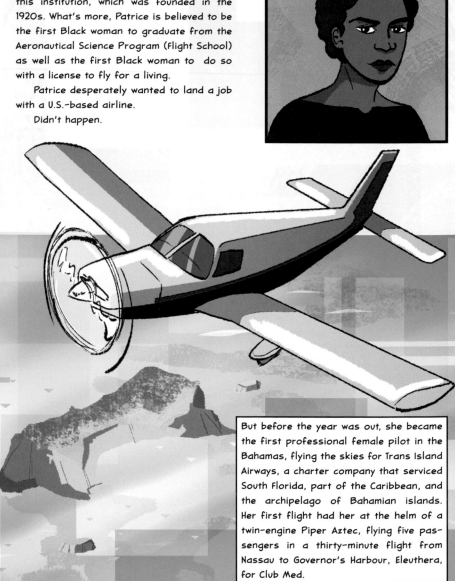

In the spring of 1982, Patrice Clarke, who looks utterly determined in her yearbook photo, graduated from Embry-Riddle with a bachelor's degree in aeronautical science and a commercial pilot's license. She was one of the first women to graduate from this institution, which was founded in the 1920s. What's more, Patrice is believed to be the first Black woman to graduate from the Aeronautical Science Program (Flight School) as well as the first Black woman to do so with a license to fly for a living.

Patrice desperately wanted to land a job with a U.S.-based airline.

Didn't happen.

But before the year was out, she became the first professional female pilot in the Bahamas, flying the skies for Trans Island Airways, a charter company that serviced South Florida, part of the Caribbean, and the archipelago of Bahamian islands. Her first flight had her at the helm of a twin-engine Piper Aztec, flying five passengers in a thirty-minute flight from Nassau to Governor's Harbour, Eleuthera, for Club Med.

As Patrice continued to fly the skies, she was having the time of her life—and she kept her cool during a mishap.

This was in 1984 when she was piloting a ten-seat, twin-engine Islander from one Bahamian island to another. Her plane was more than 5,000 feet above the waters and miles and miles away from an airport when one engine conked out.

"I HAD PASSENGERS ON THE PLANE, SO I HAD TO PRETEND I WASN'T SCARED."

Steady on she flew, looking so calm, being so brave— doing what she was trained to do, and pulling off a smooth landing on Eleuthera.

It was also in 1984 that, after more flight training and the passing of exams that certified her to
move on from flying small twin-engine aircraft to
flying turbine engine planes and jets, Patrice Clarke
became a First Officer (copilot) at Bahamasair with
its Boeings—and with her as its first female pilot!

Not every passenger was pleased about
that. When she came out of the cockpit
of a big ole Boeing, some were beyond
shocked and freaked out!

That happened less at her next job. Now she was flying primarily packages. In May 1988 she became a flight engineer for UPS Airlines, based in Louisville, Kentucky, and the eighth largest U.S. airline in the late 1980s.

With UPS Airlines, Patrice Clarke sure got to see so much more of the world—places as different as Anchorage, Alaska; Cologne, Germany; Hong Kong, China; Seoul, Korea; Sydney, Australia; and Honolulu, Hawai'i.

"WHEN I SAW THE GLACIERS FOR THE FIRST TIME MY MIND WENT BACK TO GEOGRAPHY CLASS, MY EYES WATERED, AND I WAS FILLED WITH EMOTION."

While enjoying majestic sights like Alaskan glaciers she was also dealing with some "turbulence" on the ground but she was well prepared in her craft. The challenges made her stronger.

"THE HARD TIMES WERE WHEN I STARTED TO REALIZE I WAS BEING TREATED DIFFERENTLY EITHER BECAUSE OF MY SEX AND OR BECAUSE OF MY RACE."

Once again Patrice Clarke persevered. Two years into her career at UPS she was promoted to First Officer. A few years after that, following her last flight under the scrutiny of a UPS flight-standards supervisor and a Federal Aviation Administration safety inspector, this high flier was officially upgraded to Captain—the first Black female captain for a major U.S. airline. By then she was no longer Patrice Clarke but Patrice Clarke Washington.

Months earlier she had married Captain Ray Glenn Washington, a Black pilot with American Airlines (and they became the first Black couple flying for major airlines).

The historic flight that sealed the deal on Patrice Clarke Washington's captaincy was from Miami to Atlanta on a mid-December night in 1994, with her at the helm of a DC-8, a huge four-engine jet capable of carrying three crew members, four passengers, and 100,000 pounds of envelopes thick and thin, and packages tiny and tall.

Early the next day, she was in takeoff mode again. About an hour later, she touched down in Louisville at the UPS terminal, where photographers and Captain Ray Washington were eagerly waiting for her to step off the plane.

As Captain Patrice Clarke Washington continued to fly the skies, delivering her best for UPS, when she looked back on that long-ago classroom laughter (even from her friends), she took tremendous delight in the fact that she never let that laughter bring her down.

TIMELINE

SEPTEMBER 11, 1961 born Patrice Clarke Washington in Nassau, the Bahamas.

1982 graduated from Embry-Riddle Aeronautical University and went to work for Trans Island Airways.

1984 went to work for Bahamasair.

1988 went to work for UPS Airlines as a flight engineer (the crew member tasked with managing an aircraft's various systems).

1990 promoted to first officer.

1994 promoted to captain.

1998 UPS released an ad celebrating her.

2000 received a Turner Broadcasting System Trumpet Award.

2001 retired from UPS.

2008 Inducted, along with her husband, into the Organization of Black Aerospace Professionals' Founders and Pioneers Hall of Fame.

Some Other Pioneering Pilots

★ Daredevil flier **Bessie "Queen Bess" Coleman**, a native of Texas who made Chicago home: first Black female licensed pilot (1921) and first person of color to get that license from the Fédération Aéronautique Internationale (World Air Sports Federation). Coleman had attended an aviation school in France after U.S. flight schools refused to admit her.

★ **Willa B. Brown:** first Black woman to earn her wings in the States (late 1930s, first a private pilot's license, then a commercial one) and cofounder of the first Black-owned flight school: the Coffey School of Aeronautics in Oak Lawn, Illinois (1940), where many future Tuskegee Airmen first took to the skies.

★ **Melissa "M'Lis" Ward:** first Black woman captain of a major U.S. commercial passenger airline (United in 1998). About ten years earlier, Ward had made history as the U.S. Air Force's first Black female flight instructor.

★ **Shawna Rochelle Kimbrell:** the U.S. Air Force's first Black female fighter pilot (1999).

★ **Jeanine McIntosh-Menze:** the U.S. Coast Guard's first Black female aviator (2005).

★ **Madeline Swegle:** the U.S. Navy's first Black female fighter pilot (2020).

"I really disliked *The Flintstones* because I thought that the show made fun of dinosaurs and insulted them. They didn't treat dinosaurs seriously and I thought that was a sacrilege. I would vehemently speak out against it at about age nine."

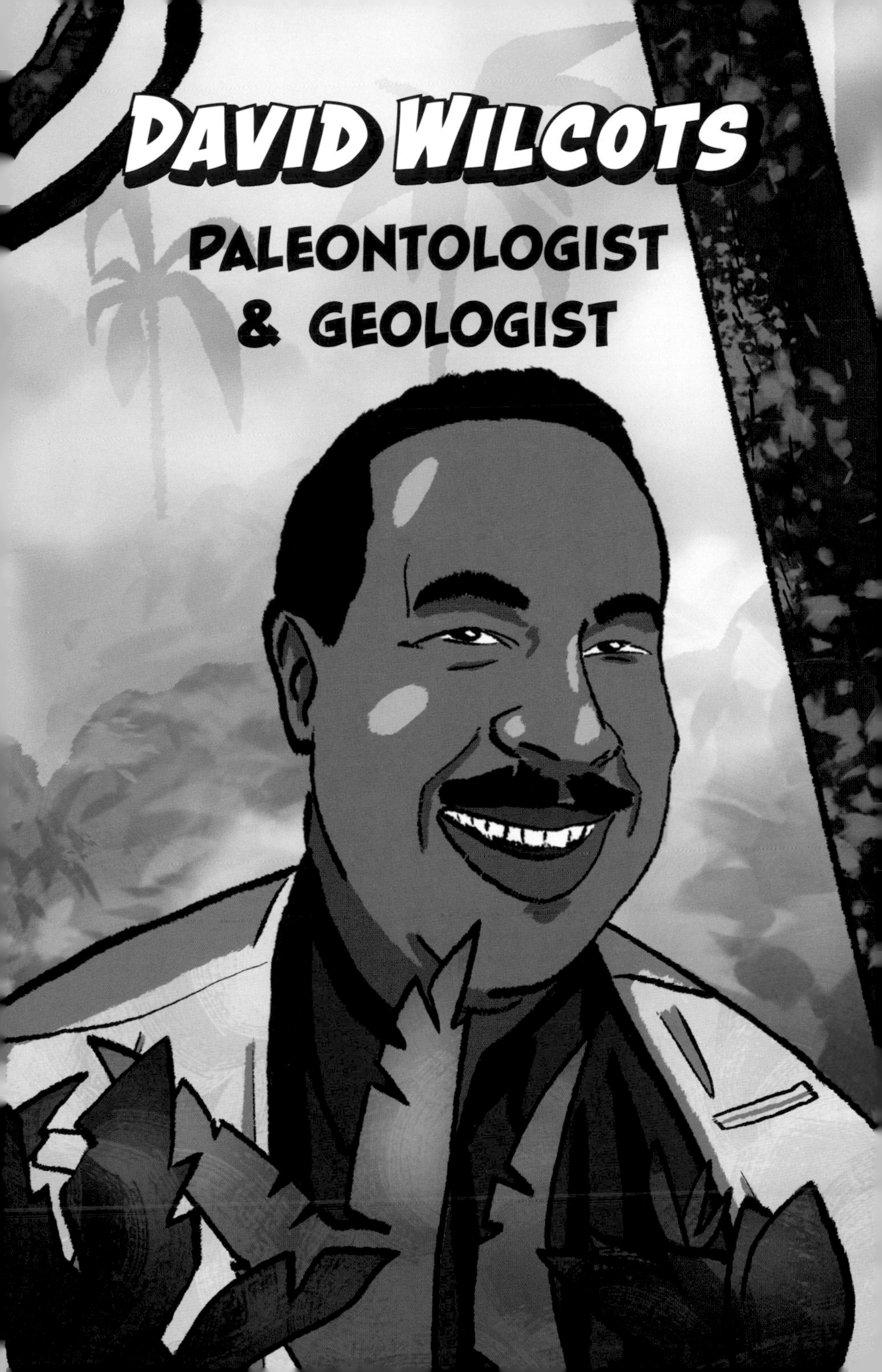
DAVID WILCOTS
PALEONTOLOGIST
& GEOLOGIST

IN THE 1960S AND 1970S, *VOYAGE TO THE BOTTOM OF THE SEA*, *WILD KINGDOM*, *WILD, WILD WORLD OF ANIMALS*, AND *UNTAMED WORLD* WERE AMONG YOUNG DAVID'S FAVORITE TV SHOWS.

David also loved visits to the Philadelphia Zoo with its elephants, giraffes, rhinos—and more!

But his all-time favorite animals were those that lived a long, long, LONG time ago—large prehistoric beasts!

"I LIKED ANY BIG MONSTER MOVIE. I LIKED *GODZILLA, MONSTER ZERO* . . . AND THAT WHOLE GENRE OF MOVIES THAT HAD BIG MONSTERS TEARING UP BIG CITIES."

He first fell in love with dinosaurs.

Like raptors with their razor-sharp teeth and a sickle-shaped claw on each foot!

Like the large, lumbering Stegosaurus with its plated back and spiky tail!

Like the ferocious T. rex with its bone-crushing bite!

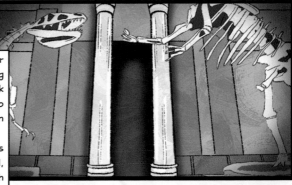

David first saw dinosaur fossils at age four, during a family trip to New York City that included a visit to the world-famous American Museum of Natural History.

Most awesome of all was the ginormous long-necked, plant-eating dinosaur with a whiplike tail that stomped around Europe and North America about 151 to 156 million years ago—an Apatosaurus (commonly called a Brontosaurus when David was a kid). When alive, this roughly 76-foot-long creature weighed about 26 tons.

After that visit to the American Museum of Natural History, David wanted to know more, *more*, and *MORE* about this and other ancient reptiles: creatures that soared through the skies, swam the seas, and ones that, like dinosaurs, roamed about on land.

I SAW THE DINOSAURS THERE AND WAS JUST TRANSFIXED. IT WAS OUT OF THIS WORLD FOR ME.

After a while, David also wanted to know more, *more*, and *MORE* about prehistoric mammals like the giant woolly rhinoceros, the saber-toothed cat, and the four-tusked elephant.

"AND THEN, WHEN I WAS IN FIFTH GRADE OR SO, I FOUND THIS BOOK IN THE SCHOOL LIBRARY CALLED *AFTER THE DINOSAURS* AND I STILL HAVE THAT BOOK."

In time, David was keen on a career in paleontology, the study of life on Earth through fossils.

"THE SCIENCE CLASSES AT PENN CHARTER WERE STRONG ALL THE WAY THROUGH. I ESPECIALLY LOVED THE EARTH SCIENCE CLASS IN EIGHTH GRADE."

The Greek palaios meaning "ancient" + Greek ŏnto meaning "creature" or "being" + Greek logia meaning "study" = **PALEONTOLOGY**.

In his quest to be a paleontologist David Wilcots earned a bachelor's degree in geology from Philadelphia's Temple University. That meant taking courses in chemistry, mathematics, physics, mineralogy, physical geology, biology—and more!

Wilcots capped that bachelor's degree with a master's degree in geology from Fort Hays State University in Hays, Kansas. His thesis was a study of the Aphelops, a long-legged, built-for-running, hornless North American rhino that lived from approximately 18 to 5 million years ago.

NEXT FOR DAVID WILCOTS?

SIBLING SCIENCE MINDS
While young David developed a passion for prehistoric life on Earth, his younger brother developed a passion for wonders far, far above. He is astrophysicist and astronomer Dr. Eric M. Wilcots at the University of Wisconsin-Madison.

Based on Wilcots's master's thesis drawings

"WHEN I GOT OUT OF GRAD SCHOOL, I LOOKED FOR JOBS IN PALEO, BUT COULDN'T FIND ANY. ENVIRONMENTAL GEOLOGY WAS THE NEXT BEST THING."

Unable to find a job in paleontology, Wilcots joined the ranks of scientists who study what's going on deep down underground so that, say, a gas company will know how and where best to build a pipeline. Investigating the contamination of soil and groundwater—and devising strategies for environmental cleanups—became one of Wilcots's areas of expertise.

"I HELPED CREATE THE MAPS THE PHILADELPHIA WATER DEPARTMENT CONSULTS IN ORDER TO FORECAST WHAT THEY WILL FIND IN A SPECIFIC SPOT IF THEY NEED TO DIG."

In the early 1990s Wilcots got a call from an American Museum of Natural History paleontologist he had gotten to know when researching the Aphelops.

Wilcots was invited to join an expedition out in Wyoming to hunt for fossils from about 47 million years ago. This was a time when forerunners of animals familiar to us today were on the scene—like horses that were two feet tall, like rhinos the size of goats.

FOSSILS are the remains or impressions of the remains of organisms preserved in rocks. The word *fossil* comes from a Latin word that means "dug up."

Wilcots went on other fossil expeditions, including ones sponsored by the Utah Geologic Survey, the University of Utah's Natural History Museum of Utah in Salt Lake City, and by the University of Washington's Burke Museum of Natural History and Culture in Seattle.

One of David's fossil finds, during a dig in Wyoming, was a skull and partial skeleton of a 47-million-year-old mammal that was related to today's pangolins (scaly anteaters).

In the summer of 2017 Wilcots spent four days on a dig in Montana. He and the rest of the crew were searching for fossils of a 66.3-million-year-old T. rex. Two years earlier, two members of a Burke Museum team had discovered it. The finds included ribs, hip bones, lower jaw bones, parts of its pelvis, and most amazing of all its 2,500-pound skull—with teeth!

More ribs and an upper arm bone are among the finds from the dig Wilcots was on in 2017.

Wilcots's passion for paleo prompted him to do volunteer work for the dinosaur lab at Philadelphia's Academy of Natural Sciences of Drexel University—educating visitors of all ages on paleontology, fossils, and dinosaurs, along with doing delicate scientific work, such as cleaning fossils and gluing broken pieces together.

He also came to enjoy making school visits, hoping to inspire young people to want to know more, *more*, and *MORE* about paleontology. In a 2017 visit to the Philadelphia School, first and second graders got to touch fossils from his own collection. One was a 130-million-year-old grapefruit-sized interior fragment of a much larger fossil dinosaur bone, possibly a thigh bone chunk.

DAVID'S FAVORITE DINO?

Kentrosaurus (ken·tro·saw·ruhs), a smaller close relation of the better known Stegosaurus. Kentrosaurus was discovered in Tanzania, East Africa, in 1921. David saw it as a kid in a book on dinosaurs given to him by his dad.

[T]HE WORLD NEEDS MORE PALEONTOLOGISTS BECAUSE WE NEED TO UNDERSTAND HOW LIFE ON THIS PLANET DEVELOPED OVER GEOLOGIC TIME.

TIMELINE

DECEMBER 5, 1961 born David Wilcots in Denver, Colorado, and spent his first two years in East Pakistan, where his architect dad, Henry Wilcots, employed by the great architect Louis I. Kahn, was designing the National Assembly Building. (In 1971 East Pakistan became the independent nation of Bangladesh.)

1963 Philadelphia became home.

1980 graduated from William Penn Charter School.

1981–1982 attended Franklin and Marshall College in Lancaster, Pennsylvania, and transferred to Temple University.

1986 earned his bachelor's in geology from Temple University.

1988 earned his master's in geology from Fort Hays State University.

1989–1992 worked as a geologist–hydrologist at Intex, Inc.

1995–1998 worked as an environmental geologist at Henkels & McCoy, Inc.

1998–2000 worked as an environmental geologist at GA Environmental Services, Inc.

2000–2002 worked as an environmental geologist at ConTech Services, Inc.

What's in a Name?

★ Raptor is short for velociraptor (vuh·**laa**·sr·ap·tr), which comes from two Latin words that translate into "speedy robber."

★ Stegosaurus (steh·guh·**saw**·ruhs) comes from two Greek words that translate into "roof lizard." (The armor plates on its back look like roof tiles.)

★ T. rex is short for *Tyrannosaurus rex* (ty·ran·no·**saw**·rus **reks**). The name comes from two Greek words that translate into "tyrant lizard" and the Latin word for "king," making the T. rex "king of the tyrant lizards."

★ Apatosaurus (uh·paa·tuh·**saw**·ruhs) comes from two Greek words that translate into "deceptive lizard."

★ Aphelops (**af**·e·lops) comes from two Greek words that translate into "smooth face."

2002–2004 worked at a geologist at Powell–Harpstead, Inc.

2004–2009 worked as a senior geologist at RMT, Inc.

2010–2012 worked as a compliance analyst at AT&T.

2012–2014 worked as a technical manager/environmental geologist at Property Solutions, Inc.

2014 became senior geologist/environmental practice lead at Sci-Tek Consultants, Inc.

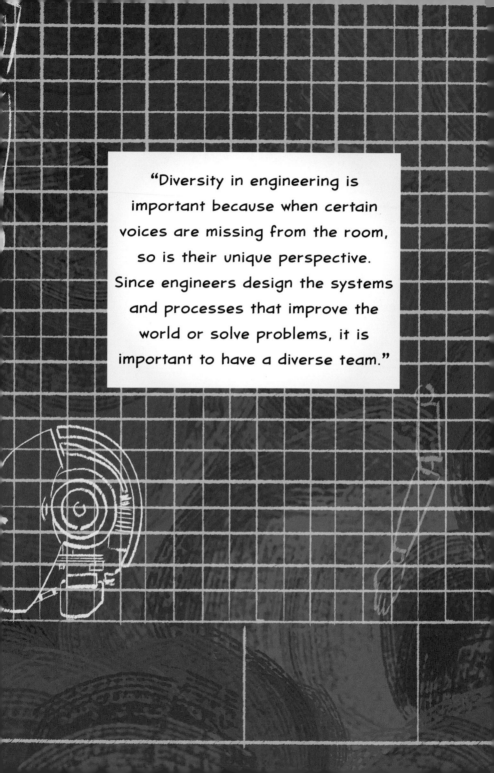

"Diversity in engineering is important because when certain voices are missing from the room, so is their unique perspective. Since engineers design the systems and processes that improve the world or solve problems, it is important to have a diverse team."

CARLOTTA A. BERRY

ROBOTICS ENGINEER

"It was probably middle school to high school when I discovered I really loved math and science."

An early victory in science came in the sixth grade when she built an electric circuit with a light bulb and a battery for the science fair.

By the time she got to high school, Carlotta's mind was made up to become a high school math teacher.

But then . . .

A guidance counselor urged her to consider becoming an engineer.

Huh?

"A train conductor?"

Engineer comes from the Latin word *ingeniator*, which comes from the Latin *ingeniare* ("to devise") and ingenium ("cleverness").

Carlotta was soon off to the library to research the field of engineering. (She couldn't google it because there was no Google—there was no internet! At least not for everyday people. This was in the 1980s.)

Of all the different branches of engineering, Carlotta lit up over electrical engineering, the branch devoted to the study, development, and testing of electrical equipment and systems, from motors and power stations to robots.

After high school, Carlotta went down to Atlanta, where she took advantage of a dual-degree program between Spelman College and Georgia Institute of Technology (Georgia Tech).

Through this program she earned two bachelor's degrees in five years: in mathematics from Spelman and in electrical engineering from Georgia Tech, where she took a robotics class. At the time, undergraduates could, sure, write code for a robot, but they couldn't touch it, only view it through a piece of plexiglass. **BUMMER!**

While at Georgia Tech Carlotta decided to become a professor of engineering.

Why?

Because she had no professors who looked like her. Also, there were very few women and Black students in the department.

> I WANTED TO CHANGE THE FACE OF ENGINEERING BY SHOWING THAT THE PROFESSION COULD BE COOL, INTERESTING, EXCITING, ENGAGING, AND, MOST IMPORTANTLY, DIVERSE.

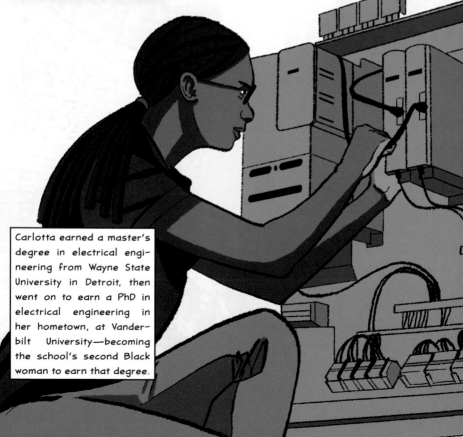

Carlotta earned a master's degree in electrical engineering from Wayne State University in Detroit, then went on to earn a PhD in electrical engineering in her hometown, at Vanderbilt University—becoming the school's second Black woman to earn that degree.

At Vanderbilt, her focus was on interactions between humans and mobile robots, including how to create robots that aren't scary and don't freak people out.

Earning those degrees wasn't easy. Carlotta was always juggling schoolwork with work-work. For example, while a Georgia Tech student, she worked at an Italian restaurant at one point. During her studies at Wayne State, she worked nights as a controls engineer for a Ford Motor Company plant, where she got to touch robots handling windshields.

"I WORKED ON THE LINE THAT ASSEMBLED THE CAR WINDSHIELDS, WHERE MY JOB WAS TO PERFORM MAINTENANCE, CODING AND UPDATES FOR THE INDUSTRIAL ROBOTS AND PROGRAMMABLE LOGIC CONTROLLERS."

"SO THAT'S WHEN MY PASSION FOR ROBOTICS WAS BORN."

After Vanderbilt, Dr. Berry taught for three years at Nashville's Tennessee State University, in its department of electrical and computer engineering. She then joined the faculty at Rose–Hulman Institute of Technology (RHIT) in Terre Haute, Indiana, to serve as a professor of electrical and computer engineering with a focus on mobile robotics, from the science behind it to design.

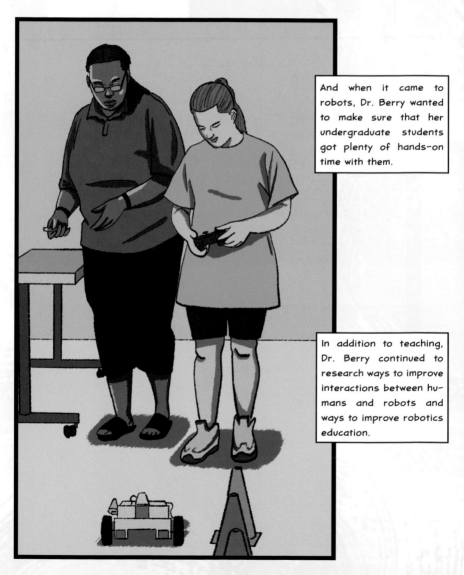

And when it came to robots, Dr. Berry wanted to make sure that her undergraduate students got plenty of hands-on time with them.

In addition to teaching, Dr. Berry continued to research ways to improve interactions between humans and robots and ways to improve robotics education.

THE GOAL IS TO DEVELOP PRINCIPLES TO ALLOW FOR NATURAL AND EFFECTIVE COMMUNICATION AND COLLABORATION BETWEEN HUMANS AND ROBOTS.

When Dr. Berry arrived at RHIT, students couldn't minor in robotics. She helped change that. Working with electrical and computer engineers, mechanical engineers, and computer science and systems engineers, she cocreated the first multidisciplinary minor-degree program in robotics.

Over the years, Dr. Berry proved to be a great encourager and inspiration to countless students with her knowledge and expertise—and with her positive energy!

"I had in my head an idea of what an engineer was, kind of very technically minded, very professional, and maybe a little bit cold," said RHIT graduate Allison Shi in 2021, "but I think that having Dr. Berry as a professor and an advisor has taught me that you can be warm and exuberant and welcoming in this field."

In her crusade for more diversity in STEM, Dr. Berry cofounded RHIT's Building Undergraduate Diversity—ROSE-BUD. This program encourages young women and people of color to enter the field of electrical and computer engineering. ROSE-BUD also offers a support system for those who do, helping them stay the course should the going get tough.

One of ROSE-BUD's initiatives is Student Projects Advocating Resourceful Knowledge—SPARK!—an annual engineering design competition for high school students. One year the challenge had to do with an egg. Teams were tasked with designing an egg-holding contraption that when dropped from a balcony wouldn't result in a smashed egg.

ROSE-HULMAN INSTITUTE OF TECHNOLOGY

In 2021 Dr. Berry was named RHIT's Lawrence J. Giacoletto Endowed Chair in Electrical and Computer Engineering for her "outstanding achievements as an educator and scholar."

Meaning?

Three years of funding for a number of initiatives, including developing an advanced course in mobile robotics and creating more outreach programs in robotics for young people.

TIMELINE

JULY 4, 1970 born Carlotta Ardell Johnson in Nashville, Tennessee.

1988 graduated from Hume-Fogg Academic High School in Nashville.

1992 earned her bachelor's in mathematics from Spelman.

1993 earned her bachelor's in electrical engineering from Georgia Tech.

1996 earned her master's degree in electrical engineering from Wayne State.

2003 earned her PhD in electrical engineering from Vanderbilt and started her career at Tennessee State.

A Few Other Engineering Minds

★ Astronomer, astrophysicist, and aeronautical engineer **George R. Carruthers** invented the first moon-based telescope, planted on the lunar surface by Apollo 16 astronauts in 1972. His telescope gave us the first images of Earth's geocorona (the outermost part of its atmosphere and made up of mostly hydrogen).

★ Computer engineer **Mark Dean** headed the team that created the IBM PC, unveiled in August 1981. It revolutionized computing in the workplace and paved the way for computers in the home, in schools—everywhere!

★ In the late 1980s electrical engineer **Jesse Eugene Russell** headed the Bell Labs team that developed digital cellular technology for the United States. He is often called the "father of 2G communications."

★ While working at Bell Labs in the 1980s, computer scientist **Marian Croak** envisioned people being able to use the internet to make phone calls. She later led the team that developed VoIP (Voice over Internet Protocol). The next time you engage with someone via Skype or Zoom, for example, give a thanks to Marian Croak, who also pioneered the technology to donate via a text.

2006 started her career at RHIT.

2018 received Leading Light Award in the category of "You Inspire Us!" from Indianapolis's Women and Hi Tech.

2021 named a distinguished Fellow by the American Society of Engineering Education (the organization's highest honor!) and received the Bridge Builder Award from the TechPoint Foundation for Youth.

2022 hailed the Society of Women Engineers' Distinguished Engineering Educator of the Year.

"Evolutionary biology is a very diverse field . . . Its basic question is how did the diversity of life on earth arise? . . . It's basically focused on the mechanisms by which new species arise, the mechanisms by which animals and plants and fungi and other things come to have the appearance that they do, what we call the phenotype."

SCOTT V. EDWARDS
ORNITHOLOGIST

IN A JULY 2020 INTERVIEW HE SAID THAT HE WAS NINE OR TEN WHEN A NEIGHBOR IN THE RIVERDALE SECTION OF THE BRONX, NEW YORK, TOOK HIM BIRDWATCHING. QUICKLY, YOUNG SCOTT WAS HOOKED ON BIRDING!

THE "SPARK BIRD" FOR ME WAS THE NORTHERN FLICKER, OR WHAT WE USED TO CALL A YELLOW-SHAFTED FLICKER. I COULDN'T BELIEVE THAT SOMETHING SO GAUDY AND OUTRAGEOUS IN A FIELD GUIDE COULD BE IN MY BACKYARD.

At the time of the interview Scott Vernon Edwards was enjoying a cross-country bike trip, from Massachusetts to Oregon—and by then he was so much more than a birdwatcher.

He had become a prominent, award-winning ornithologist, specializing in evolutionary biology—studying the diversity of birds; analyzing bird habitats, past and present; probing into things like the origins of feathers and how emus, ostriches, and other flightless birds came to be. (By then, he had also appeared in the documentary miniseries *Beast Legends*, an exploration of mythological beings, including the griffin, a fearsome creature with a lion's body and an eagle's head, wings, and talons.)

ORNITHOLOGY (or·nih·thaal-uh·jee) comes from the Latin word ornithologia, which comes from the Greek words ornis ("bird") and logia ("study").

WAVE HILL

Evolving from a birdwatcher to a bird scientist wasn't something young Scott ever dreamed of. Birding was just a hobby.

It had him heading out on long walks in search of feathered friends.

It had him poring over Peterson Field Guides so that he could identify birds he spotted on the wing or perched in a tree.

That hobby also had Scott signing up for an internship in the summer of 1981 at Wave Hill, a public garden and cultural center in Riverdale. His work included writing *Second Sightings: A History of Ornithology in Riverdale, New York*, a booklet for an exhibit of paintings of birds. Scott worked at Wave Hill shortly after he graduated from Phillips Exeter Academy in Exeter, New Hampshire, where he happened to have a biology teacher who was a birder.

In the fall of 1981, Scott was off to Harvard University in Cambridge, Massachusetts. Early on he planned to major in the history of science. He also toyed with the idea of becoming a doctor like his dad.

After a stressful sophomore year, Scott took a break. But he didn't just laze about the house. He was on the move!

He went down to Washington, D.C., where he volunteered at the Smithsonian National Museum of Natural History—cataloging bones, pitching in on research, learning about museum work.

Scott left the museum after about six months because of a chance encounter with an awesome article in *Natural History* magazine by ornithologist C. John Ralph.

"IT HAD AMAZING PHOTOS OF HAWAIIAN FOREST BIRDS."

Scott had the gumption to write to Ralph. He asked if he could join him in studying birds in Hawai'i, where, it just so happened, Scott had lived as a baby. As for C. John Ralph, he was no longer in Hawai'i but he was good enough to put Scott in touch with folks who took him on as a volunteer.

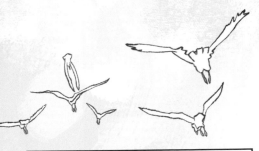

While on Hawai'i's Big Island, Scott had incredible experiences—ones that had him seeing the place in a whole new light!

"WE WERE AT ABOUT 4,000 FEET IN VOLCANOES NATIONAL PARK IN HAWAI'I, AND IT SORT OF BLEW APART ALL MY MYTHS ABOUT WHAT HAWAI'I WAS LIKE. YOU MIGHT IMAGINE HAWAI'I AS, YOU KNOW, BEACHES AND PALM TREES . . . VERY TROPICAL."

But there was nothing at all very tropical about where he stood.

"IT WAS COOLER, VERY GREEN, AND OFTEN FOGGY."

Scott also helped out with bird surveys atop Mauna Kea, the tallest mountain in the world, from its underwater base to its summit. At nearly 10,000 feet above sea level—where it was sunny but cool—the team studied the palila, a rare honeycreeper. While in Hawai'i, Scott also studied albatrosses and other seabirds on tiny Tern Island.

A few years later, Scott graduated from Harvard magna cum laude with a bachelor's in biology. He soon went west to earn a PhD in zoology from the University of California, Berkeley. His focus: the DNA of songbirds.

Fieldwork included spending four months in the eastern mountains of Papua New Guinea researching bowerbirds and birds-of-paradise.

That fieldwork also included spending ten months in Australia studying its songbirds, especially the grey-crowned babbler.

After he earned his PhD, this recipient of a prestigious Alfred P. Sloan research fellowship went south to the University of Florida in Gainesville. There, for two years in the early 1990s, he worked under an eminent zoologist and a renowned immunologist, studying wild birds and the evolution of their disease-resistance genes.

ZOOLOGY comes from the Latin zoologia, which comes from the Greek words zoion ("animal") and logia ("study").

Being in Gainesville came with the big bonus of being able to observe long-legged spoonbills and other wild birds he'd never see up North. He also delighted in sightings of chubby manatees.

Dr. Scott V. Edwards next journeyed to the Pacific Northwest, to Seattle, to be assistant professor of zoology at the University of Washington and to also serve as curator at its Burke Museum of Natural History and Culture, that held about 150,000 specimens of birds from all over the world.

After nine years in Seattle, he went back east, back to Harvard, where, in addition to being a professor, he became curator of ornithology at the university's Museum of Comparative Zoology, with its roughly 400,000 bird specimens.

And, yes, Dr. Edwards's work continued to include travel—taking students on field trips to places as different as Mongolia, Panama, and Costa Rica.

Biking across America had been on Dr. Edwards's bucket list for years, a dream he couldn't fulfill because of his busy schedule. Then came the COVID-19 pandemic in early 2020.

Classes canceled.
    Conferences canceled.
    Fieldwork canceled.
    Now he had the time for that epic bike ride.
    He set off on June 6 after giving the tires of his brand-new Surly a quick dip in the Atlantic Ocean at Plum Island in Newburyport, Massachusetts.

> "I WAS EXCITED TO SEE A FAMILY OF WESTERN FLYCATCHERS, THE UPLAND SANDPIPERS WERE SUPER COOL, AND WHEN I SAW YELLOW-HEADED BLACKBIRDS I ALMOST FELL OFF MY BIKE."

During his trip, Dr. Edwards had the thrill of experiencing the sights and sounds of a "changing birdscape."

A northern bobwhite in upstate New York . . . horned larks in Ohio . . . a red-headed woodpecker in Illinois . . . winter wrens in Idaho . . . brown creepers in Oregon.

On August 20, 2020, Dr. Edwards dipped his bike in the Pacific Ocean at Sunset Beach, Oregon. He had pedaled through 15 states on a 76-day, 3,800-mile journey—and only had three flat tires!

After a rest up at a seaside hotel, the brilliant, intrepid, fun-loving Dr. Scott Vernon Edwards boarded a great big, beautiful metal bird that flew him home.

BLACK LIVES MATTER

TIMELINE

JULY 7, 1963 born Scott Vernon Edwards in Honolulu, Hawai'i, where his dad, an army doctor, was stationed.

1971–1978 attended The Buckley School on Manhattan's Upper East Side, not far from New York Hospital, where his father worked. (His mother, a lawyer, also worked in Manhattan.)

1981 graduated from Phillips Exeter Academy.

1986 earned his bachelor's in biology from Harvard.

1992 earned his PhD in zoology from the University of California, Berkeley, followed by postdoctoral studies at the University of Florida, Gainesville (completed in 1994).

1995 began his career at the University of Washington.

2003 began his career at Harvard.

2006 elected a fellow of the American Ornithologists' Union.

2009 elected a fellow of the American Academy of Arts and Sciences and of the American Association for the Advancement of Science.

ALSO FOR THE BIRDS

J. Drew Lanham sees "conserving birds and their habitat" as "a moral mission," one "that needs the broadest and most diverse audience possible to be successful." A birder as a boy growing up on his family's farm in Edgefield, South Carolina, Lanham earned a bachelor's and master's in zoology and a PhD in forest resources from Clemson University, where he eventually became Alumni Distinguished Professor of Wildlife Ecology, Master Teacher, and Certified Wildlife Biologist. His 2016 book, *The Home Place: Memoirs of a Colored Man's Love Affair with Nature*, won a Southern Book Prize. In 2022 Dr. Lanham was one of the twenty-five people to receive a MacArthur Award from the John D. and Catherine T. MacArthur Foundation. The award, commonly called the "genius award," came with a grant of $800,000.

2015 received the Elliott Coues Award from the American Ornithological Society and elected to the National Academy of Sciences, the most prestigious U.S. scientific society.

2019 awarded the Molecular Ecology Prize.

2020 won the first Inclusiveness, Diversity, Equity, and Access (IDEA) Award from the Society for the Study of Evolution.

2022 elected to Sweden's Royal Physiographic Society of Lund (also known as the Academy for the Natural Sciences, Medicine and Technology).

" I actually never wanted to be a
day-to-day marine biologist . . .
in a lab all day . . . or even scuba
diving every day . . . I wanted to
understand the ocean well enough
to read everyone else's papers
and figure out how we can use all
that information to protect and
restore the ocean for all the
folks that rely on it. "

Ayana Elizabeth Johnson

MARINE BIOLOGIST

"FISH, FISHING, DIVING AND THE MANAGEMENT OF CORAL REEFS."

This is the title of the 200-plus-page dissertation Ayana Elizabeth Johnson produced while earning her 2011 PhD in marine biology from the Scripps Institution of Oceanography, a department of the University of California, San Diego.

Research for that dissertation included spending splendid days in the Caribbean designing a fish trap that would reduce bycatch, that is, catch fisherfolk don't want because no one will buy it. Examples of bycatch include juvenile fish about the size of a finger (and called fingerlings). There's also the reef-dwelling narrow-bodied surgeonfish, more popular as an aquarium fish than as food.

The trap that Johnson designed had "escape gaps" that allowed many, many fingerlings to flee and maybe live long enough to reproduce. Many, many escaped surgeonfish could go about their important work of eating algae off coral reefs and thereby keeping reefs healthy.

Winner of the 2012 Rare's Solution Search

With her PhD in hand, this native of Brooklyn, New York, who had earned a bachelor's degree in environmental science and public policy from Harvard and who had served as a policy advisor for major agencies, including the National Oceanic and Atmospheric Administration—well, Dr. Johnson stayed busy, busy, busy working on ocean care and raising awareness of how to "use the ocean without using it up."

In 2013, Dr. Johnson became executive director of the Waitt Institute, which works with governments on sustainable ocean management.

At Waitt, Dr. Johnson cofounded and led the Blue Halo Initiative, which focused on ocean care in the Caribbean. The pilot program was on Antigua's sister island, tiny Barbuda. Its waters were in serious trouble!

IT'S NOT LIKE IT USED TO BE.

Algae smothered its coral reefs!
So much of the coral was dead! Palastar Reef, once so glorious, had become "a graveyard of coral skeletons, and a ghost town with few fish." Its stock of conch, lobster, and fish was shockingly low, forcing fisherfolk to go farther and farther out to make a living.

After working closely with government officials and getting tons of input from community leaders and everyday Barbudans—especially fisherfolk—Blue Halo banned the catching of parrotfish and sea urchins.

Like surgeonfish, they keep coral reefs from being smothered by algae and dying. Dead coral reefs can't absorb particles and keep the waters clear and clean; can't provide food for fellow creatures; and can't offer hiding places for baby shellfish and finfish, thus preventing them from being all gobbled up by a shark or other predator.

Blue Halo Barbuda also created sanctuary zones—areas closed to fishing so that fish could replenish. Fishing in the majestic Codrington Lagoon, for example, was prohibited for two years. With its coral reefs, mangroves, and seagrasses, the lagoon is a vital habitat and nursery for lobster along with silvery tarpon and other finfish.

Worldwide coral reefs are home to about 25 percent of all marine life.

In 2015 the Waitt Institute launched Blue Halo Montserrat and Blue Halo Curaçao.

In her ocean activism, Dr. Johnson took to authoring and coauthoring a bunch of scientific papers and policy papers—on coral reef degradation and coral reef restoration, for example.

She also took to blogging. Posts include:
- "We Need to Kick Our Addiction to Plastic"
- "Solving Humanity's Grand Challenges Requires a Healthy Ocean"
- "To Save Coral Reefs, Start with Parrotfish"

In April 2017 she founded Ocean Collectiv, a consulting firm on ocean conservation. About ten months later she cofounded Urban Ocean Lab, a think tank promoting environmental justice for coastal cities, which face rising sea levels and more devastating storms year after year.

When she learned of the Green New Deal, an action plan to seriously address climate change, Dr. Johnson was as happy as a clam. But when she read the actual proposal congressional Democrats drafted, she was shocked to see that the oceans got short shrift. She became a leading voice in the call for a Blue New Deal to go alongside the Green New Deal. In 2020 she coauthored a Blue New Deal plan for presidential candidate Senator Elizabeth Warren.

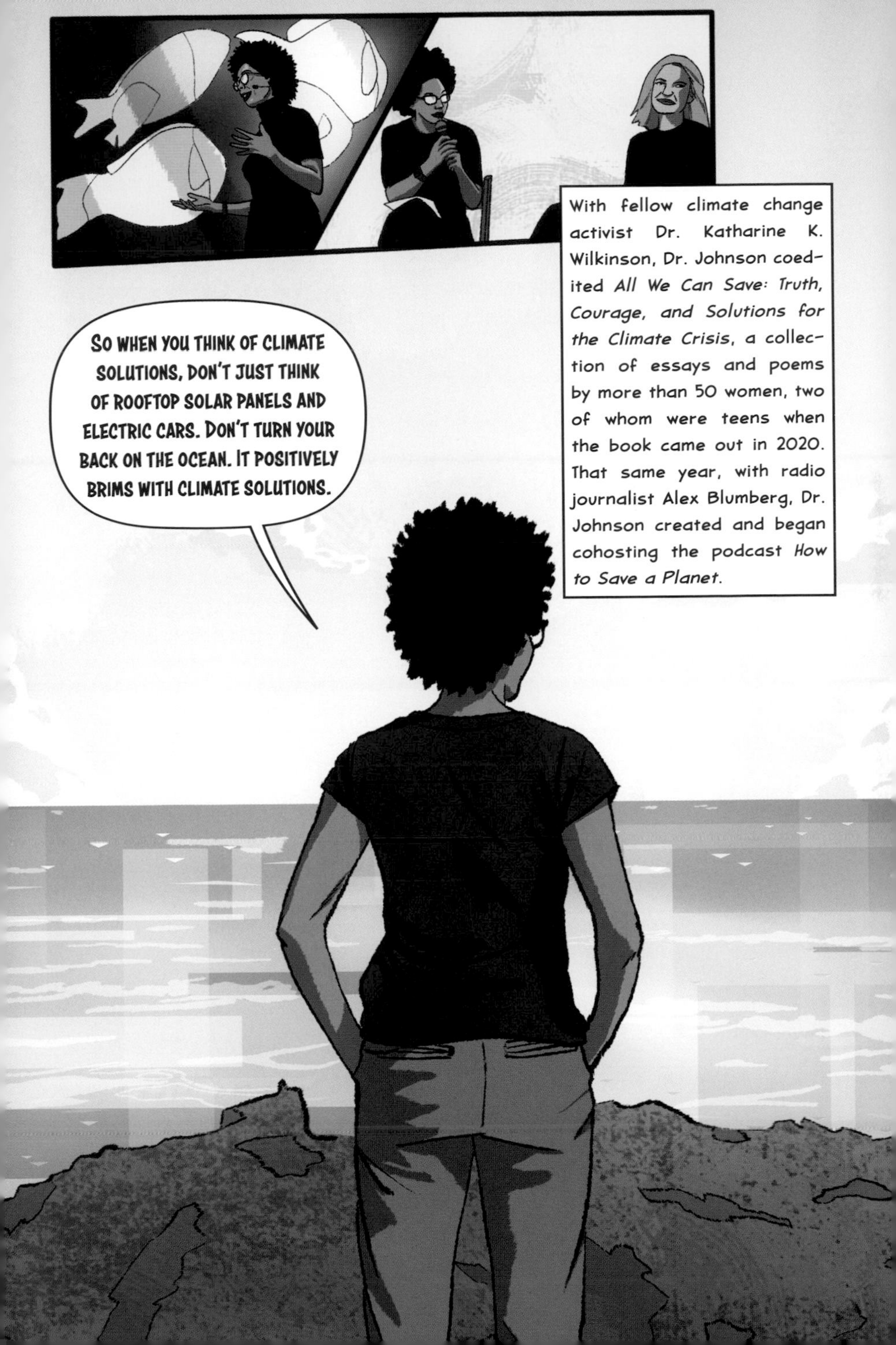
With fellow climate change activist Dr. Katharine K. Wilkinson, Dr. Johnson coedited *All We Can Save: Truth, Courage, and Solutions for the Climate Crisis*, a collection of essays and poems by more than 50 women, two of whom were teens when the book came out in 2020. That same year, with radio journalist Alex Blumberg, Dr. Johnson created and began cohosting the podcast *How to Save a Planet*.
SO WHEN YOU THINK OF CLIMATE SOLUTIONS, DON'T JUST THINK OF ROOFTOP SOLAR PANELS AND ELECTRIC CARS. DON'T TURN YOUR BACK ON THE OCEAN. IT POSITIVELY BRIMS WITH CLIMATE SOLUTIONS.

Not surprisingly, Dr. Johnson became a leading go-to person for talks and interviews on the damage done to oceans and the consequences. Such as the heating up of the waters. Such as sea level rise. Such as acidification.

A LOT OF SPECIES ARE MIGRATING TOWARDS THE POLES TO TRY TO FIND COOLER WATERS. WARMER WATER HOLDS LESS OXYGEN, SO FISH ARE HAVING TROUBLE BREATHING.

WE HAVE CHANGED THE PH OF SEAWATER GLOBALLY BY HOW MUCH CARBON DIOXIDE WE'VE FORCED IT TO ABSORB. FOR CORAL AND SHELLFISH THAT'S A REAL THREAT.

Solutions?

More offshore wind farms.

Preserving and restoring coral reefs, mangroves, seagrasses, and wetlands to lessen the force of storm surges and the flooding it causes—much cheaper, she says, than building seawalls.

THE OCEAN IS ACTUALLY EXPANDING AS IT HEATS UP. SEA LEVEL RISE MEANS THAT STORM SURGES ARE BIGGER.

"THROUGH PHOTOSYNTHESIS AND THE FORMATION OF SHELLS, OCEAN FARMS ABSORB TONS OF CARBON . . . A SINGLE ACRE OF OCEAN CAN PRODUCE 25 TONS OF SEAWEED AND 250,000 SHELLFISH IN FIVE MONTHS."

"OFFSHORE, THE WIND BLOWS MORE STRONGLY AND CONSISTENTLY THAN IT DOES OVER LAND, SO FLOATING TURBINES COULD MEAN MORE ENERGY, GENERATED MORE RELIABLY."

ALL WE CAN SAVE

ALL WE CAN SAVE

And there's regenerative ocean farming: underwater gardens of shellfish and the superfood kelp—gardens that can feed a whole lot of people and help with the problem of overfishing.

As is the case with other science minds you've met in this book, Dr. Johnson's passion can be traced back to a childhood experience. She fell in love with the ocean at age five during a family vacation in Key West, Florida, where her parents taught her to swim. Most wondrous of all was a ride in a glass-bottom boat. Little Ayana Elizabeth was dazzled by all that she saw down below, most especially a coral reef.

"I HAD A PRIVATE VIEW OF THIS UNDERWATER MAGICAL WORLD."

TIMELINE

AUGUST 23, 1980

born Ayana Elizabeth Johnson in Brooklyn, New York.

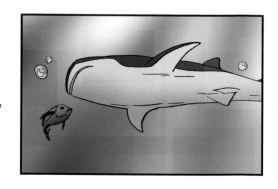

1998 graduated from Brooklyn's Berkeley Carroll School.

2002 earned her bachelor's in environmental science and public policy from Harvard.

2011 earned her PhD in marine biology from Scripps Institution of Oceanography.

2013–2016 served as executive director of Waitt Institute.

2017–2019 was an adjunct professor at New York University.

2017 founded Ocean Collectiv.

2018 cofounded Urban Ocean Lab.

2021 received the Stephen H. Schneider Award for Outstanding Climate Science Communication.

2022 appointed to a three-year term as the Roux Distinguished Scholar at Bowdoin College.

NOTES

*In a few instances dialogue was created based on facts and original sources as indicated in the endnotes.

MATILDA EVANS

"The health of a people is that people's wealth": Darlene Clark Hine, "The Corporeal and Ocular Veil: Dr. Matilda A. Evans (1872–1935) and the Complexity of Southern History," *The Journal of Southern History*, 70, no.1 (February 2004): 28.

"steeping leaves to make medicines": "The Story of a Negro Child's Resolve," *The Youth's Instructor*, May 18, 1909, 7.

Courses Evans took at WMCP: Report card Woman's Medical College of Pennsylvania for Miss M.A. Evans for 2nd year and 3rd year, Dr. Matilda A. Evans Collection, Smithsonian National Museum of African American History and Culture, sova.si.edu/details/NMAAHC.A2019.109#ref2.

Number of women doctors ca.1897: "History of Women in Medicine," Office of Diversity and Inclusion, Heersink School of Medicine, University of Alabama, Birmingham, www.uab.edu/medicine/diversity/initiatives/women/history. According to this article, the United States had more than 7,000 women doctors. They made up about 5.5 percent of all the nation's physicians.

Evans's fees, house calls, and first car: Burnett W. Gallman Jr., MD, "Dr. Matilda Arabella Evans," Smithsonian National Museum of African American History and Culture, transcription.si.edu/project/36169.

"I have done well": "Letter from Matilda Evans to Alfred Jones, March 13, 1907, Legacy Center Archives and Special Collections, Drexel University College of Medicine, doctordoctress.org/islandora/object/islandora:971/story/islandora:421#page/1/mode/2up.

"South Carolina's brainiest . . . around Columbia" and "a half dozen eggs": "South Carolina's Brainiest Negro," *The State*, January 10, 1910, 3.

On the clinic's first few days: "Clinic Doing Good Work Among Negroes of City," *The State*, October 29, 1931, 3.

"The health conditions": "Matilda Arabelle Evans, MD," Columbia City of Women, www.columbiacityofwomen.com/honorees/matilda-arabella-evans-md.

"an all costuming passion": "Columbia Clinic to Enlarge Endeavors," *Palmetto Leader*, March 14, 1931, 8.

"The rooms and furnishings": "Clinic Doing Good Work Among Negroes of City," *The State*, October 29, 1931, 3.

On adoptions and foster parenting: Darlene Clark Hine, "The Corporeal and Ocular Veil: Dr. Matilda A. Evans (1872–1935) and the Complexity of Southern History," *The Journal of Southern History*, 70, no.1 (February 2004): 23.

ARCHIE ALEXANDER

"First comes the dream.": Elizabeth Murphy Oliver, "The Man Iowa Did Not Want," *Afro-American*, *Afro Magazine* section, October 20, 1956, 5.

Alexander's height and weight: Richard H. Weingardt, "Archibald Alphonso Alexander," *Leadership and Management in Engineering*, 9, no. 4 (October 2009): 208.

"Never mind that the dean": This is based on his statement: "The dean of the school of engineering said to me that it would be pretty hard for me to find work as an engineer and that it was a waste of time," in Elizabeth Murphy Oliver, "The Man Iowa Did Not Want," *Afro-American*, *Afro Magazine* section, October 20, 1956, 5.

"Never mind that a professor told me that": This is based on the following passage: "Engineering is a tough field at best," the professor pointed out, "and it may be twice as tough for a Negro," in "Bridge Builder Alexander Bucked Prejudice and Won the Hard Way," *Chicago Defender*, April 24, 1943, 3.

"When I was a little boy": Elizabeth Murphy Oliver, "The Man Iowa Did Not Want," *Afro-American, Afro Magazine* section, October 20, 1956, 5.

Required courses: Bulletin of the State University of Iowa, June 1909, 334–35.

Alexander's thesis: The title is "The design for a reinforced concrete viaduct for College Street, Iowa City, Iowa." It is in the University of Iowa's Engineering Bachelors Theses Collection, aspace.lib.uiowa.edu/repositories/3/archival_objects/243466.

"I did it!": This is based on Alexander's obvious determination and the fact that earning an engineering degree was a dream come true for him. How proud he was to earn his degree in civil engineering. Presumably to the professor who discouraged him, Alexander said, "I am sure that I can make the grade." From "The Man Who Said 'I Can,' and Did It," *Afro-American*, May 23, 1931, 20.

Alexander's earnings at Marsh's firm: Jack Lufkin, "Archibald Alphonse Alexander (1888–1958)," *African American Architects: A Biographical Dictionary, 1865-1945*, edited by Dreck Spurlock Wilson (New York: Routlegde, 2004), 12.

repairing a chimney: "The Man Who Said 'I Can,' and Did It," *Afro-American*, May 23, 1931, 20.

small paving jobs: "Negro Engineer Completing $2,500,000 Construction Job at University of Iowa," *Sunday Gazette and Republican* (Cedar Rapids, IA), June 19, 1927, section 3, 1.

Passport application: Ancestry.com., U.S., Passport Applications, 1795–1925 [online database], Ancestry.com Operations, Inc., 2007.

Higbee's injuries: Ancestry.com., U.S., Death Records, 1880–1904, 1921–1952 [online database], Ancestry.com Operations, Inc., 2017.

"all the machinery . . . gleam in his eyes": "Negro Engineer Completing $2,500,000 Construction Job at University of Iowa," *Sunday Gazette and Republican* (Cedar Rapids, IA), June 19, 1927, section 3, 1.

"leading contract engineers in Iowa and the Midwest": "Negro Engineer Completing $2,500,000 Construction Job at University of Iowa," *Sunday Gazette and Republican* (Cedar Rapids, IA), June 19, 1927, section 3, 1.

Number of alums honored and the number of graduates: "Archibald A. Alexander," Iowa College of Engineering, engineering.uiowa.edu/alumni/awards/honor-wall/distinguished-engineering-alumni-academy-members/archibald-alexander.

"high attainment in their chosen fields of endeavor": "99 Alumni Honored for 'High Attainment,'" *Daily Iowan*, June 8, 1947, 7.

"That was the proudest moment in my life": Elizabeth Murphy Oliver, "The Man Iowa Did Not Want," *Afro-American, Afro Magazine* section, October 20, 1956, 5.

Middle name: On his World War I and World War II draft registration cards, his middle name is "Alfonso." Ancestry.com., U.S., World War I Draft Registration Cards, 1917-1918 [online database], Ancestry.com Operations Inc, 2005 and Ancestry.com., U.S., World War II Draft Registration Cards, 1942 [online database], Ancestry.com Operations, Inc., 2010. At some point, "Alphonso" became the standard spelling. Some sources use "Alphonse."

Home at 2200 Chautauqua Parkway: Renda Lutz, "House Was Center of Dispute," *Des Moines Register*, February 16, 2000, 3AT–WN.

FRED JONES

"There are three ways for you to become successful": Virginia Ott and Gloria Swanson, *Man with a Million Ideas: Fred Jones Genius/Inventor* (Minneapolis: Lerner Publications, 1977), 109.

On his place of birth: Some sources say that he was born in Covington, Kentucky. His World War I and World War II registration draft cards have Cincinnati, Ohio, as his birthplace. Ancestry.com., U.S., World War I Draft Registration Cards, 1917–1918 [online database], Ancestry.com Operations Inc, 2005 and Ancestry.com. U.S., World War II Draft Registration Cards, 1942 [online database], Ancestry.com Operations, Inc., 2010.

"If you want to eat, you work!": Gloria M. Swanson and Margaret V. Ott, *I've Got an Idea!: The Story of Frederick McKinley Jones* (Minneapolis: Runestone Press, 1994), 11.

sedan and touring car: Steven M. Spencer, "Born Handy," *Saturday Evening Post*, May 7, 1949, 153.

"And I remember it was a Friday": Steven M. Spencer, "Born Handy," *Saturday Evening Post*, May 7, 1949, 153.

chicken disaster: Smithsonian Institution, *Smithsonian Makers Workshop: Fascinating History & Essential How-Tos: Gardening, Crafting, Decorating & Food* (Boston: Houghton Mifflin Harcourt, 2020), 130.

"I half expected that old boiler to blow up": Swanson and Ott, *I've Got an Idea!*, 23.

"If you guys can cool off a big movie theater . . . knocks the whole thing apart": Ott and Swanson, *Man with a Million Ideas*, 77.

"A big clunk": Swanson and Ott, *I've Got an Idea!*, 65.

"More than 5000 trucks and trailers": "Steven M. Spencer, "Born Handy," *Saturday Evening Post*, May 7, 1949, 155.

"for outstanding achievements": "Award to Be Given," *Minneapolis Star*, February 26, 1953, 12.

GLADYS B. WEST

"It's strange": Brittney Kinsey, "Calculating the Future: STEM Pioneer Gladys West Overcomes Segregation," Dvidshubs.net, www.dvidshub.net/news/270710/calculating-future-stem-pioneer-gladys-west-overcomes-segregation.

"He even related it to farming": Gladys B. West with M. H. Jackson, *It Began with a Dream* (King George, VA: IGWEST Publishing, 2020), 31.

"college material": West with Jackson, *It Began with a Dream*, 31.

"I was told by my teachers": Brittney Kinsey, "Calculating the Future: STEM Pioneer Gladys West Overcomes Segregation," Dvidshubs.net, www.dvidshub.net/news/270710/calculating-future-stem-pioneer-gladys-west-overcomes-segregation.

"This machine, the size of an entire room": West with Jackson, *It Began with a Dream*, 63.

I never stopped one moment: Aamna Mohdin, "Gladys West: The Hidden Figure Who Helped Invent GPS, *The Guardian*, November 19, 2020, www.theguardian.com/society/2020/nov/19/gladys-west-the-hidden-figure-who-helped-invent-gps.

PATRICE CLARKE WASHINGTON

"I wanted to fly airplanes": Lisa Lansman, "'Women and Flight' Shows Female Side of Aviation History," *The Dispatch and Rock Island Argus*, March 5, 2001, B5.

"Even my friends laughed.": "Soaring to New Heights," *Ebony*, July 1995, 74.

"Whatever had to be done": "Soaring to New Heights," *Ebony*, July 1995, 76.

"She remembers being so mesmerized": "Soaring to New Heights," *Ebony*, July 1995, 76.

"My family flew a lot": Rodney Ho, "Pilot Inspires Others to Follow Her Lead," *The Atlanta Journal/The Atlanta Constitution*, January 25, 1995, D3.

Description of first day at Embry-Riddle: Patrice Clark Washington, comment to author, November 9, 2023.

"My God, what have I gotten myself into?": Patrice Clarke Washington, email to author, November 9, 2023.

Sampling of courses: Patrice Clarke Washington, email to author, November 9, 2023.

"I had passengers on the plane": Ben Z. Hershberg, "History-Making UPS Captain Is Flying High," *Courier-Journal* (Louisville), December 27, 1994, A4.

"When I saw the glaciers": Joan Oleck, "Washington, Patrice Clarke 1961–," Encyclopedia.com, https://www.encyclopedia.com/education/news-wires-white-papers-and-books/washington-patrice-clarke-1961.

"The hard times were": Joan Oleck, "Washington, Patrice Clarke 1961–," Encyclopedia.com, https://www.encyclopedia.com/education/news-wires-white-papers-and-books/washington-patrice-clarke-1961.

The numbers: Rodney Ho, "Pilot Inspires Others to Follow Her Lead," *The Atlanta Journal/The Atlanta Constitution*, January 25, 1995, D3 is the source for the numbers about UPS pilots. The July 1995 *Ebony* article said that there were eleven Black women pilots working for major airlines (p. 74).

"I never let that incident": "Soaring to New Heights," *Ebony*, July 1995, 74.

DAVID WILCOTS

"I really disliked *The Flintstones*": David Wilcots, email to author, November 6, 2023.

"I liked any big monster movie": Tatiana Bacchus, "Black Sci-Fi Talks to Paleontologist David Wilcots," BlackSci-Fi.com, September 22, 2015, blacksci-fi.com/black-sci-fi-talks-to-paleontologist-david-wilcots/.

"I saw the dinosaurs there and": "Interview with Paleontologist: David Wilcots," PrehistoricBeastoftheWeek.blogspot.com, December 19, 2020, prehistoricbeastoftheweek.blogspot.com/2020/12/interview-with-paleontologist-david.html.

"And then, when I was in 5th grade or so": Tatiana Bacchus, "Black Sci-Fi Talks to Paleontologist David Wilcots," BlackSci-Fi.com, September 22, 2015, blacksci-fi.com/black-sci-fi-talks-to-paleontologist-david-wilcots/.

"The science classes at Penn Charter": Julia Judson Rea, "Subterranean Adventures: Dave Wilcots OPC '80," *Penn Charter Magazine*, Fall 2016, 11.

"When I got out of grad school": Thea Boodhoo, "Down to Earth With: Geologist and paleontologist David Wilcots," EarthMagazine.org, May 1, 2018, www.earthmagazine.org/article/down-earth-geologist-and-paleontologist-david-wilcots/.

"I helped create the maps": Julia Judson Rea, "Subterranean Adventures: Dave Wilcots OPC '80," *Penn Charter Magazine*, Fall 2016, 11.

Wilcot's find in Wyoming: Alumni Class Notes, *Penn Charter Magazine*, Fall 2014, 44.

Visit to the Philadelphia School: "Cretaceous Age Enters the Classroom," December 3, 2017, www.tpschool.org/blog/2017/12/3/tsftso1alfet6kmvzivldcx4ocv53o.

"[T]he world needs more paleontologists": "Interview with Paleontologist: David Wilcots," PrehistoricBeastoftheWeek.blogspot.com, December 19, 2020, prehistoricbeastoftheweek.blogspot.com/2020/12/interview-with-paleontologist-david.html.

CARLOTTA A. BERRY

"Diversity in engineering is important": "Exploring human-robot interaction and bringing people together through robotics—Dr Carlotta Berry, Professor in Electrical and Computer Engineering at Rose-Hulman Institute of Technology," Womanthology.co.uk, June 23, 2021, womanthology.co.uk/exploring-human-robot-interaction-and-bringing-people-together-through-robotics-dr-carlotta-berry-professor-in-electrical-and-computer-engineering-at-rose-hulman-institute-of-technology/.

"It was probably middle school to high school": Sue Loughlin, "Rose-Hulman Prof Is Changing the Face of Engineering," *Tribune-Star*, April 9, 2021, tribstar.com/news/local_news/rose-hulman-prof-is-changing-the-face-of-engineering/article_7fdc60a1-cc49-53a8-8446-d7b33bfda44e.html.

"A train conductor?": This is based on Dr. Berry's statement that, after being encouraged to become an engineer, "I had to go to the library and look it up in a book because, back then, an engineer was a train conductor in my mind." In Rina Diane Caballar, "Work of Art," Prism.org, November 2022, asee-prism.org/up-close-fall/.

"I wanted to change the face of engineering": Our Stories, "Carlotta Berry Honored for STEM Advocacy and Named Endowed Engineering Chair," Spelman.edu, June 2021, spelman.edu/about-us/news-and-events/our-stories/stories/2021/06/07/carlotta-berry-honored-for-stem-advocacy-and-named-endowed-engineering-chair.

"I worked on the line": "Exploring human-robot interaction and bringing people together through robotics—Dr Carlotta Berry, Professor in Electrical and Computer Engineering at Rose-Hulman Institute of Technology," Womanthology.co.uk, June 23, 2021, womanthology.co.uk/exploring-human-robot-interaction-and-bringing-people-together-through-robotics-dr-carlotta-berry-professor-in-electrical-and-computer-engineering-at-rose-hulman-institute-of-technology/.

"So that's when": Moser Consulting, "S1E10: Dr. Carlotta Berry of the Rose-Hulman Institute Discusses Diversity in Science, Technology, Engineering, and Mathematics," March 3, 2021, *ASCII Anything I*, podcast, 02:50.

"The goal is to develop": Carlotta A. Berry, "Robotics Engineer Interview for HS Students," NoireSTEMinist.com, July 2, 2021, noiresteminist.com/post/robotics-engineer-interview-for-hs-students.

"I had in my head an idea . . . welcoming in this field": Allison Shi, " 'It Is Not Just a Man's Field': Avon Woman Changing the Face of Engineering, Rose-Hulman Professor Paving Pathway for More Diversity," WRTV.com, wrtv.com/news/hiring-hoosiers/education/it-is-not-just-a-mans-field-avon-woman-changing-the-face-of-engineering.

"outstanding achievements": "Carlotta Berry Named Giacoletto Endowed Faculty Chair," News & Events, Rose-Hulman.edu, April 7, 2021, rose-hulman.edu/news/2021/carlotta-berry-named-giacoletto-endowed-faculty-chair.html.

SCOTT V. EDWARDS

"Evolutionary biology is a very diverse field": Scott Edwards (The HistoryMakers A2012.171), interviewed by Larry Crowe, October 12, 2012, The HistoryMakers Digital Archive. Session 1, tape 5, story 1, Scott Edwards provides an overview of evolutionary biology.

"The 'spark bird' for me": Hillary T., "In Your Words: Scott V. Edwards," *Your Great Outdoors* (Mass Audobon blog), September 22, 2020, blogs.massaudubon.org/yourgreatoutdoors/in-your-words-scott-v-edwards.

"It had amazing photos of Hawaiian forest birds": Scott Edwards (The HistoryMakers A2012.171), interviewed by Larry Crowe, October 12, 2012, The HistoryMakers Digital Archive. Session 1, tape 4, story 2, Scott Edwards describes his ornithology-based study in Hawai'i.

"We were at about 4,000 feet": Scott Edwards (The HistoryMakers A2012.171), interviewed by Larry Crowe, October 12, 2012, The HistoryMakers Digital Archive. Session 1, tape 4, story 2, Scott Edwards describes his ornithology-based study in Hawai'i.

"It was cooler": Scott V. Edwards, email to author, February 8, 2024.

"About two weeks before my departure date": Scott V. Edwards and as told to Latria Graham, "Millions Took to the Streets to Fight Racial Injustice. I Rode Across America," Bicycling.com, December 3, 2020, bicycling.com/culture/a34721652/scott-edwards-bike-america/.

On flat tires: Bridget Alex, "Journey Complete, Scott Edwards Looks Back on His Cross-Country Bicycling Trip," Audubon.org, August 27, 2020, audubon.org/news/journey-complete-scott-edwards-looks-back-his-cross-country-bicycling-trip.

"changing birdscape": Lauren Daley, "Going the Distance," *Boston Globe*, July 4, 2020, C10.

"I was excited to see a family of Western Flycatchers": Hillary T., "In Your Words: Scott V. Edwards," *Your Great Outdoors* (Mass Audubon blog), September 22, 2020, blogs.massaudubon.org/yourgreatoutdoors/in-your-words-scott-v-edwards/. With edits by Scott V. Edwards sent to author, November 11, 2023.

"conserving birds . . . diverse audience possible to be successful": Dr. Roger Lederer, "Birding While Black," Ornithology.com, June 1, 2020, ornithology.com/birding-while-black/.

AYANA ELIZABETH JOHNSON

"I actually never wanted to be a-day-to-day marine biologist": Ali Pattillo, "How a Young, Black Marine Biologist Turned Her Imposter Syndrome into Real Change," Inverse.com, October 5, 2020, inverse.com/mind-body/ayana-elizabeth-johnson.

"I designed these fish traps": Ayana Elizabeth Johnson, "Solution: Escape Gaps for Fish Traps," AyanaElizabeth.com, May 7, 2013, ayanaelizabeth.com/nat-geo-8.

"use the ocean without using it up": Ayana Elizabeth Johnson, "How to Use the Ocean Without Using it Up," AyanaElizabeth.com, February 22, 2017, ayanaelizabeth.com/nat-geo-45.

"a graveyard" and "It's not like it used to be": Ayana Elizabeth Johnson, "Blue Halo Barbuda: Using the Ocean Without Using it Up," AyanaElizabeth.com, January 14, 2014, ayanaelizabeth.com/nat-geo-19.

"A third of Americans live in coastal cities": "An Interview with Ayana Elizabeth Johnson," *Journal of International Affairs*, vol. 73, 1 (Fall 2019/Winter 2020): 243.

"So when you think of climate solutions": Ayana Elizabeth Johnson, "To Save the Climate, Look to the Oceans," *ScientificAmerican.com* (blog), June 8, 2020, blogs.scientificamerican.com/observations/to-save-the-climate-look-to-the-oceans/.

"A lot of species are migrating": "An Interview with Ayana Elizabeth Johnson," *Journal of International Affairs*, vol. 73, 1 (Fall 2019/Winter 2020): 246.

"We have changed the pH: "An Interview with Ayana Elizabeth Johnson," *Journal of International Affairs*, vol. 73, 1 (Fall 2019/Winter 2020): 246.

"The ocean is actually expanding": "An Interview with Ayana Elizabeth Johnson," *Journal of International Affairs*, vol. 73, 1 (Fall 2019/Winter 2020): 246.

"Offshore, the wind blows": Ayana Elizabeth Johnson, "To Save the Climate, Look to the Oceans," *ScientificAmerican.com* (blog), June 8, 2020, blogs.scientificamerican.com/observations/to-save-the-climate-look-to-the-oceans/.

"Through photosynthesis": Ayana Elizabeth Johnson, "What I Know About the Ocean," SierraClub.org, December 12, 2020, sierraclub.org/sierra/future-oceans-environmental-justice-climate-change.

"I had a private view": Bonnie Tsui, "Ayana Elizabeth Johnson Is the Climate Leader We Need," OutsideOnline.com, October 31, 2020, outsideonline.com/outdoor-adventure/environment/ayana-elizabeth-johnson-climate-change-leader/.

"Octopuses—they have three hearts and are extremely intelligent": Stephanie Granada, "Meet the Most Influential Marine Biologist of Our Time," OutsideOnline.com, August 29, 2017, outsideonline.com/outdoor-adventure/environment/meet-most-influential-marine-biologist-our-time/.

ACKNOWLEDGMENTS

Big thanks to our editor, Maggie Lehrman, for bringing us together—and for her excellence throughout the entire process! For your equally wonderful work we thank you managing editor Marie Oishi, assistant managing editor Kayla White, copyeditor Diane Aronson, designer Charice Silverman, and design manager Andrea Miller.

Tonya also thanks University of Iowa folks who were so helpful in her research on Archie Alexander: Bailey Adolph, Katie McCullough, Denise Anderson, Jan Brunstein, and Meaghan Lemmenes.

And thank you, Patrice Clarke Washington, David Wilcots, and Dr. Scott V. Edwards, for your generous responses to my queries.

Last but not least, Tonya is ever grateful to her agent, Jennifer Lyons, for all that she does on her behalf.

David sends thanks to Tonya Bolden, James Burns, Emily Fernandez, Charice Silverman, and Maggie Lehrman.